THE

HAPPY

HIGHWAYS

"In the Highlands of Staffordshire"

Revisited by

Ray Poole

© Ray Poole and Churnet Valley Books
ISBN 1897949 40 5
1998

Samuel Sigley & Sons

Funeral Directors

Est 1869

Lyndhurst House
Queen Street
Leek
Staffordshire
ST13 6LS

tel. 01538 382048

Greystones

17th Century Tea Room

Greystones is a delightful Grade II* listed building. Its mullioned windows and leaded lights provide the perfect setting for morning coffee, lunch and afternoon tea. The proprietress, Janet, takes care of all the baking and her cakes have attracted a devoted following. Located on Stockwell Street, next to the Library, Greystones is open from 10am to 5pm on Tuesday, Wednesday, Friday & Saturday.........................Tel: 01538 398522

W H Nithsdale's photograph of Three Shire Heads

THE HAPPY
HIGHWAYS

A journey through the
Staffordshire Moorlands
in the footsteps of
W H Nithsdale

CHURNET VALLEY BOOKS

CHURNET VALLEY BOOKS
PUBLISHERS OF LOCAL HISTORY
43 BATH STREET
LEEK, STAFFS ST13 6JQ
Tel: 01538 399033   Fax: 01538 399696

Titles of local interest published by Churnet Valley Books and currently available include:-

EARTH MYSTERIES OF THE THREE SHIRES   Doug Pickford
THE WARDLE STORY   Anne Jacques
COUNTRYWISE   Raymond Rush
RUDYARD LAKE 1797-1997   Basil Jeuda
HISTORY OF THE BATHS AT BUXTON   Langham & Wells
HISTORY OF HORTON HALL   J F Moxon
HISTORY OF THE 2nd LEEK SCOUTS   ed. Basil Turner
A PINT-SIZED HISTORY OF THE
STAFFORDSHIRE MOORLANDS   Joan-Ann Grindley

FACSIMILE REPRINTS
OLDE LEEK VOL II (1900 edition)   M H Miller
TALE OF IPSTONES (1937 edition)   Rev F Brighton
CHEDDLETON - A VILLAGE HISTORY   ed. R Milner
THE OLD ROAD TO ENDON (1974 edition)   ed. R Speake
HISTORY OF CHEADLE (1881 edition)   Robert Plant
IN THE HIGHLANDS OF STAFFORDSHIRE   W.H.Nithsdale

Enquiries are
invited with

regard to publishing
proposals

Dedication

During the writing of this book our elder son, David, died at his home in Australia - 12,000 miles away from the Staffordshire Moorlands where he grew up.

He loved these hills, moors and dales. The local countryside was a significant part of his early life.

These were his 'happy highways' also, which we shared together during the years of his youth. And because of his deep affection for the area, which neither distance nor death can destroy, we believe that he is still a part of the Spirit of the Moorlands. So, David, this is your book.

Sermons in Stone - moorland stiles
The stile on the the right is an old stone 'squeezer', flanked by its modern wooden counterpart.

Preface

TO ACCOMPANY A FAMOUS TRAVELLER on his journeys is a privilege denied to most of us. However, with a little imagination on the part of the reader, this book attempts to do just that.

The Staffordshire Moorlands has never been devoid of chroniclers of the changing scene. Poets, historians, travellers and naturalists have written about the district, and have left a rich heritage, but alas, many of their works are now out of print. I first discovered W.H.Nithsdale's little book, 'In the Highlands of Staffordshire' many years ago, and over the years, through many a re-reading, and the discovery of his wonderfully evocative photographs, I have come to regard him as an old friend. What better companion, then, for a journey around the Staffordshire Moorlands than W.H.Nithsdale?

Mr.Nithsdale was the agent for the Inland Revenue in Leek during the Edwardian years. He was in the area for only a few years, but during his short time in Leek he developed a great love for the district, and he was able to use his twin talents of writing and photography to leave a lasting testimony of that love. Nithsdale was a Scotsman, and you can almost hear his lilting Scottish brogue coming through the pages of his delightful little travelogue. When the book was first published in 1906 Leek was a prosperous little township, still basking in the glory of its Victorian 'golden years', and he has given us a very vivid and lively account of his impressions, written in the form of excursions awheel and afoot throughout the area, usually by pony and trap or by bicycle.

Mr.Nithsdale will be our companion as we relive those outings of long ago, seeking both the changing and the enduring aspects of the moorlands. Relevant extracts from his book are included, but the original book should be read in full to enjoy its rich flavour. Nithsdale's sharp wit and keen observation have been my inspiration, a peg, so to speak, on which to hang my own descriptions, memories and thoughts. And like Nithsdale, I have included a story or two here and there, for the area has many, and some of the yarns about the great 'characters' of the district are apocryphal.

If, dear reader, I have caused offence to anyone, my sincere apologies, for no offence is intended. Whilst writing about the Staffordshire Moorlands many memories have come flooding back to me - memories of growing up in Leek, memories of my first discoveries of the more remote parts of the moorlands, memories of school days and boyish pranks, memories evoked by the area in which I was born and grew up. I have written about the Staffordshire Moorlands from my own individual viewpoint. This is the moorlands area as I know it, and as I remember it. The views expressed are my own, and any errors herein are entirely mine. So this is not just another book of local history, although much history can be found within its pages.

It does not aim to be a closely-researched, scholarly book, and it should not be read as such. A lot of the history here is legend, folk lore or local tradition, for the heritage of any area abounds in this type of story. We are always keen to conserve and protect the visible remains of our past, such as our old buildings. We should be equally keen to preserve those unseen and intangible aspects of our history - its stories and traditions.

Neither is this a guide book, although anyone who wishes can follow the journeys described, as the roads are all good routes for the motorist or cyclist. Also, throughout the area there are many footpaths and tracks, interlacing the district and opening up the splendid moorland countryside to the walker. A number of these tracks are ancient highways, or early trade routes, which would be traversed by packhorse or stage coach.

Nor is this a topographical account of the Staffordshire Moorlands, although the land, its people, its past and its present form the backbone of the book, and the industries and activities of man which have shaped the landscape and environment over many hundreds of years play an important role in these memories. Nithsdale's excellent photographs greatly enhance his original book. He had a rich talent for spotting the unusual view, and managed to capture much of the real spirit of the moorlands in his pictures - an aspect often missed by commercial postcard producers today. I hope that my own efforts to emulate the camera work of my alter-ego will serve to present a few late-Twentieth Century views of the Moorland scene.

Nithsdale's original book contained a number of contemporary advertisements. We have sought to emulate this, to produce the same number of pages, and a similar blend and feel of advertisers. To this end many of the advertisements are for the same businesses or very similar ones in the area. I am grateful to the current advertisers for their support which has also allowed the book to be sold for less.

And the Happy Highways of the title? This is part of a favourite quotation from A.E.Houseman's 'A Shropshire Lad', to which due acknowledgement is given. These verses seem to express so much of my own feelings about the Staffordshire Moorlands:

> Into my heart an air that kills
>> From yon far country blows.
> What are those blue remembered hills,
>> What spires, what farms are those?
>
> This is the land of lost content,
>> I see it shining plain,
> The happy highways where I went,
>> And cannot come again.

CONTENTS

Hanging Stone. Swythamley.

ACKNOWLEDGEMENTS

I have found much inspiration in other Victorian and Edwardian guidebooks, notably Edward Bradbury's 'All about Derbyshire' (1884), the North Staffordshire Railway's official illustrated guidebook, 'Picturesque Staffordshire' (1908), and The Official Illustrated Guide to the North Staffordshire Railway by George Moores (1891) plus, of course, Miller's 'Olde Leeke' (1897 and 1901), and Sleigh's History of Leek, the old standard works on Leek's history. Dr. Robert Plot's 'The Natural History of Staffordshire' (1686) is unique in the annals of early county histories, and this, too, has been widely consulted.

Thanks are expressed to All Saints Church, Leek, for permission to quote from John Betjeman's guide to the church, which is available at the church, and to the Rev. Michael Fisher for the little extract from Heath's diary relating to the building of the church. Many people have told me stories as we have gone about the moorlands, and I am grateful to my friends in the Leek Historical Society and Leek Field Club, and others too numerous to mention by name, for some of these.

A copy of the poem "Kingsley Church", by Abraham K.Moseley, was given to me by Mrs Anne Senior (formerly Moseley) and I am grateful for her permission to reproduce verses from it.

Robert Milner and his father before him have always been knowledgeable and informative companions along the way. My uncle, Percy Poole, has a great fund of stories about old times around Ball Haye Green, and I am grateful to him. George Bowyer, Geoffrey Fisher, George Short and Basil Jeuda have often sparked off thoughts, particularly when looking at old photographs and postcards.

And finally, these happy highways have been made all the happier by having my wife and family as companions on so many of them.

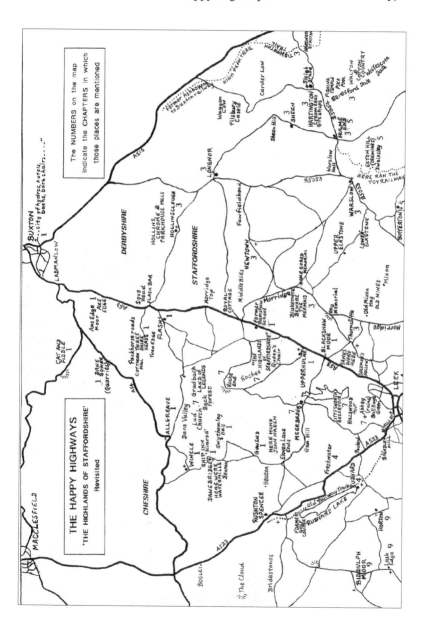

Three Shire Heads - a modern riding school follows the ancient packhorse route

CHAPTER I

ROUND THREE SHIRE HEADS
By Upperhulme, Middlehills, Flash, Buxton, Dane Bower,
Allgreave, Wincle, Danebridge, Swythamley and Gun End

NITHSDALE, MY OLD FRIEND, perhaps I may call you 'WH' as together we retrace your excursions around the Staffordshire Moorlands? These 'happy highways' are precious to both of us. I shall value your company and your observations as we relive those years of 'lost content' in the light of the many changes. And, like all good companions on the road, we'll share a few memories and a few stories along the way.

We become immediately aware of one change, as we consider our transport options today. We now take the motor car for granted, we are slaves of the internal combustion engine; we bow to the gods of speed, comfort and convenience, and our obsession with the automobile means that we miss so much of the world around us. To fully appreciate the flavour of the Staffordshire Moorlands we need to savour it gently, like a good wine, and allow its magic to work upon us. You and your companions, my friend, were fortunate. With your friend Wilkinson and his young daughter Jessie, your transport was the bicycle and the pair-horse landau. What a splendid way to tour the Moorlands! Riding in the open-air with the keen, fresh moorland wind in your face you were a veritable 'king of the road.' Furthermore, you were 'environmentally friendly', and if, at this stage of the Twentieth Century, we could all follow your modes of transport, we would have plenty of time to reflect, to muse and to contemplate the beauty of these Highlands.............

We drove up the Buxton Road enjoying an extensive panorama on our left; and beyond an interesting old toll-house, with a grand prospect of moorland before us, we drove down a slope, and then down a steep incline into Solomon's Hollow.

And so we are on our way, leaving Leek by the Buxton Road, and passing on the right the neat little drinking fountain, with its splendid pediment in nicely-dressed stone, still standing today as a fine example of the stonemason's craft, and a reminder of olden days when it would have watered many a weary traveller on the challenging road to Buxton. The Victorians were very fond of drinking fountains, and our towns and parks abound with them, symbols of the Victorian ideals of health and clean living. Nowadays we take for granted the pure, clear drinking water brought to our homes at the turn of a tap, but these surviving items of street furniture remind us of the days when this essential daily need was supplied by these drinking fountains, wells and springs - and there were no water rates to pay then!

The 'extensive panorama on the left' to which you referred is now the Haregate Housing Estate. The earlier parts of the estate were planned between the two world wars by W.E.Beacham, architect to the Leek Urban District Council - the local government authority at the time, for this is largely a council estate. The area was designated as the Abbottsville, Novi Lane and Haregate Housing Schemes, and local people who were lucky enough to be allocated a house were said to be living 'up the scheme'. This urban expansion was continued in the 1950s when the post-war housing boom pushed the boundaries of Leek outwards, encroaching on the surrounding countryside, and to commemorate the new Elizabethan Age, the roads and streets were given names with a regal ring - Windsor Drive, Prince Charles Avenue and Queens Drive.

Down to the left, among the houses, is the little junior school of St Paul's, also known as the Beresford Memorial School in memory of a former vicar who was a local historian. Once surrounded by open fields, it is now in the midst of a housing estate. I wonder if the Big Ship still sails on the Ally-ally-o down there in the playground? Do they still know how to chalk out the pattern of a hop-scotch game? And is Ring-o-ring-o-roses still played in its old traditional form? Or have children's street games changed along with their changing fashions in dress, music and entertainment?

Alas, the school children can no longer scamper up the field to the Buxton Road, as we did during the war years, to raise our snotty little noses over the stone boundary wall and watch with excited interest the American soldiers marching to or from the military base at Blackshaw Moor, some three miles up the road. Our hopes of receiving some of the luxuries which were denied to us by the austerity of the war years were rarely disappointed and we were regaled with sweets, chocolate, fruit or that item forever associated with the 'Yanks' - chewing gum. Whenever we heard the chorus of 'hup-two-three-four, one-two-three-four' drifting up the road we knew that the Americans were on their way, and in our fertile young imaginations, stimulated by the silver screen, we expected to see *real* film stars amongst them.

The little brook which used to run alongside Novi Lane beyond the school has also now been lost to building developments. Here we would fill our jam jars with frog-spawn in the spring. Then, with great interest and excitement, we would peer into the murky water in the jar, waiting for the little black dots to grow an elongated 'tail' as they gradually turned into tadpoles. Collecting tiddlers and other things in jam jars was a great pastime in those days, and what we managed to get into our jars was truly amazing - the whole incredible world of creation in microcosm, all there in half a pint of muddy water, opening our childlike eyes to the wonders of the world of nature. Simple, uncomplicated pleasures. This was the brook where, in the summer, we would paddle, and create, with the ingenuity of childhood, splendid works of civil engineering in miniature - dams, reservoirs and waterfalls - using the stones and sticks which lay around. Here in the winter we would make holes in the ice, and roll huge snowballs to block what little water might be flowing. Each season the brook had its own attractions, and all our various extra-mural activities, in the changing seasons of the year, meant that we usually arrived home soaking wet, to the chagrin of our parents, and a good telling off; but what a magic and exciting world 'that damn brook' encompassed.

Novi Lane was unsurfaced in those days, and was frequently muddy, so we rarely arrived at school with clean shoes, much to the annoyance of our headmaster, Mr.Berridge, a strict disciplinarian, but a fine teacher, although we did not always fully appreciate this at the time. His frequent cleanliness campaigns often found us falling short of his high standards. He was one of those rather old-fashioned teachers who always commanded respect.

The origin of the name 'Novi' is a matter for speculation. It was one of the roads made out of the Common Lands in 1811, when it was known as Ball Haye Green Road. The most likely explanation of the name 'Novi' is associated with the silk industry. 'Novi' silk came from a town of that name in northern Italy, where silk weaving was the main industry, as it was in Leek at that time..

SO ON WE GO, UP THE BUXTON ROAD, straight as an arrow, aiming towards the distant high moors, past the 'little toll-house', standing proudly by the roadside, a reminder of the era of turnpike roads. Then, on the left, we pass the Waste. This small, pleasantly-wooded area, enclosed by stone walls, deserves a better name, but it is common land, providing a little retreat between the main road and the Haregate housing estate, and a shelter from the cold moorland winds which sweep down from the north. To generations of children it has served as a battlefield over which many rough-and-tumble 'wars' have been fought, with wooden 'guns'. It was our Sherwood Forest and it stood for the plains of the American West, outlaws behind every tree, pursued by Roy Rogers and Trigger. Or perhaps our own little Alamo, or the El Dorado that few of us ever found.

You could always get the very best conkers from the Waste. Come September and the annual hunt would be on to find the biggest, the hardest, the shiniest, and then it was home and into the oven for the final hardening. But there was a great skill in hardening conkers, you had to get it just right - too much fire and the conker would become brittle, and shatter at the first hefty whack from your opponent, who would then add one more notch to his tally. A good conker, however, would carry you through many battles, and your 'fifty-sixer' would be vastly superior to your opponent's 'twenty-fiver.' And you were regarded with awe and reverence if you managed to notch up a century! What a pity if modern technology, with its video and computer games, forces conkers into oblivion, for it is a great tradition.

But children grow up quickly, and then the Waste might become the place where you took your first sweetheart, a quiet paradise for courting couples 'walking out' hand-in-hand. It is then, perhaps, when the children have gone home and left the Waste to the young lovers, that its trees become more sinned against than sinning! To the older generation, the Waste has always been a gentle place for a stroll with the dog, to sit and smoke your pipe and watch the world go by, or a short cut to the hospitality and a welcome pint at the Moss Rose Inn, a hostelry on the fringe of Leek, which is therefore neither a town nor a country pub, but enjoys the best of both worlds.

A SUDDEN BEND in the road and a steep descent and we are in Solomon's Hollow. Just why the name of the old King of Israel, renowned for his wisdom, should be perpetuated in this moorland location is not clear. The most likely explanation lies in the fact that much of the land hereabouts was once owned by a man named Solomon Ash. An air of mystery and romance is brought to Solomon's Hollow by the ancient story of marital infidelity, jealousy and murder recorded in Miller's 'Olde Leeke':

> It was in the time of Henry, son of William the Conqueror, that Liulph of Alderley, suspecting that his wife was not faithful to him, and being told that she had left her home, set off at once and crossed the Lime or boundary, and after searching for a long time found her, not far from home, in a lonely place now called Solomon's Hollow, near Tittesworth with his kinsman Gamel of Tettesworth; and in his rage killed the latter without giving him a chance to defend himself.

It is an all too familiar story, as old as the time of man, and one which would have called for the wisdom of a Solomon to pass judgement upon. The article in 'Olde Leeke', contributed by Gustavus Sneyd, concludes:

> Considering the facts, and the arguments which I think may be fairly drawn from them, and keeping in mind the situations of Alderlee, Solomon's Hollow, and Tittesworth, and also that the Lime which the murderer is said to have crossed, probably means that he crossed.........the Churnet, I cannot resist the opinion that this old tradition is indeed worthy of belief.

Some of these conclusions may be somewhat tenuous, in the manner of many of these old historians, who often stretched a point to make a point! But it all makes interesting reading, and adds to the folklore of the area. And have we the wisdom of a Solomon to pass a judgement?

BLACKSHAW MOOR. Its name conjures up a picture of the bleak, wild moorlands - the romance of a Brontë novel, or the mystery of a Sherlock Holmes story. But we have not yet reached the higher moors - the 'Highlands of Staffordshire', to use your expression, my friend, and we are still in the more gentle farming country to the north of Leek.

Blackshaw Moor has memories of a different kind. During the Second World War a small town of rapidly-constructed prefabricated Nissen huts sprang up, almost overnight, like the mushrooms which used to abound in the area. These were the billets to house the American servicemen, frequently referred to as 'over paid, over sexed and over here'. This 'Little America', so suddenly transplanted in the Staffordshire Moorlands, did much to foster Anglo-United States relationships during those dark days of the war, as the female population of the area discovered, often to their pleasure, and sometimes to their distress! Young girls' heads were turned and hearts melted in response to their whistles and calls, and they learned new and exciting dance routines. What Moorlander, before this American invasion, had heard of the 'jitterbug'? Many experienced their first romantic affairs, and in due course a new female phenomenon emerged - the GI Bride. American slang expressions found their way into the vocabulary of the local schoolchildren, and the old traditional North Staffordshire dialect became peppered with such phrases as 'Hey, Baby', 'Got any gum, chum?' and 'Hiya, Buddy, put it there'. There were a number of places in the area where the Americans were billeted, but Blackshaw Moor was the main centre. Many lasting friendships were formed, and the GIs were made welcome with local families, where they found a warm home-from-home. The dances at the camp were great social occasions, and properly chaperoned parties of local girls were able to make home seem perhaps not quite so far away for many of the soldiers.

This was the second time in less than 150 years that Leek experienced a foreign 'invasion' of hot-blooded young bucks from overseas. The first occasion was during the Napoleonic Wars, 1803-1814, when French prisoners-of-war were sent to Leek 'on parole'. They were housed in the local community, and although they had to observe certain disciplines and attend a daily muster, they were allowed a good deal of freedom of movement within the confines of the town. We can draw certain parallels between the two events, because these Frenchmen too, were able to fraternise with the young ladies of the town who would no doubt welcome these handsome young foreigners with romantic sounding names with open arms. Some met and married local girls and settled in the town to bring up their families. Other relationships may well have been as passionate but were not so permanent. It seems clear that there is likely to be more French and American blood in the local populace than is usually admitted. A few Italian prisoners of war also stayed at the camp, but their freedom was more restricted.

Towards the end of the war, the Americans were followed by the Polish soldiers and refugees. Many of these had experienced a hard war, and much suffering, and their rather dour outlook was in great contrast to the cavalier and devil-may-care attitude of the Americans. Nevertheless, they found a very warm welcome in the local area, once the language barriers had been broken down, and they became gradually integrated into the community. At the end of the war, many were unable to return home, indeed most had lost their homes and families entirely during the war. A small housing estate was established opposite the Three Horse Shoes, providing comfortable permanent homes for these embryonic Polish families. This 'Little Poland' in the Staffordshire Moorlands had its own Roman Catholic church and priest. Eventually local industry was able to utilise their various talents and engineering skills, and the Moorlands area has been greatly enriched by their presence.

BUT I DIGRESS, WH, and we must now return to our route, and follow you to Upperhulme.

Upperhulme, we discovered nestling Swiss-like beneath these formidable Rocks and Roches. It has a dye-house, the first of a number engaged in Leek's silk industry, on the Churnet. We made a detour here to visit Leek's water-works, a few hundred yards up the valley, behind the village. They proved to have been a most inexpensive undertaking; just a small circular tank, fed by a series of springs, which, in the driest of seasons, have never yet failed.

The modest 'water-works' which you observed, WH, in the early years of the century, are now long redundant, but in their day they were very important to the town of Leek, providing, in Victorian times, a much-needed water supply. Their significance prompted William Challinor, a Leek solicitor, to commemorate the event by presenting to the town in 1876, the Challinor Fountain. The fountain, a highly-regarded piece of Victorian sculpture, was the work of Joseph Durham, RA. Mr. Challinor saw it on exhibition at the Royal Academy in London, purchased it, and it was erected on its original site in Leek Market Place on 9 December 1876, where it stood until 1924 when it was moved to Brough Park. It now enhances the forecourt of Moorlands House, the offices of Staffordshire Moorlands District Council. In recent times one of the figures lost its head as a result of an act of vandalism, but this has now been sculptured anew, and looks none the worse.

Upperhulme itself has changed very little from your time, my good friend. The main road, since it was re-aligned, and the Twentieth Century, have largely by-passed it, and this little cluster of stone-built houses nestling by the ford in the shadow of the Roches has retained much of its old-world character. Upperhulme was granted two of the essential elements of all moorland villages, perhaps you would agree - a chapel and a pub. The chapel was built in 1838, and incorporated a Sunday School. Typically of moorland Methodism, it was, at its founding, supported mainly by a single family, the Rogers family. The pub, formerly named the New Inn, was the meeting place for the Ancient Order of Foresters (Court No.1427 Colliers' Refuge), a Friendly Society, one of many such societies which flourished in the moorland villages, providing people, for a modest weekly subscription, with some financial help in times of sickness and need, before the days of the Welfare State. The New Inn has now been re-named Ye Olde Rock Inn, in deference to its rugged setting.

Upperhulme was the site of the former Tatton's dye works, which you observed on your original visit. In 1869 William Tatton of Buxton Road, Leek, purchased the disused water-powered flax mill at Upperhulme, and furnished it for his trade of silk-dyeing, borrowing £370 to do so. With his initial workforce of nine local men in this isolated moorland spot William Tatton embarked on an enterprise that would continue well into the Twentieth Century, with factories in Leek and beyond - a major contributor to the local economy.

Today Upperhulme stands as the 'Gateway to the Roches'. Now here I must be pedantic, and insist that we must carefully note the spelling of 'Roches' - NOT 'Roaches'. A roach is a fish! Dr Robert Plot noted this in his 'Natural History of Staffordshire', published in 1686:

> When I came to Leeke and faw the Hen-Cloud, and Leek Roches, I was quickly undeceived, though my admiration was ftill heighten'd to fee fuch vaft rocks and fuch really ftupendous Profpects, which I had never feen before, or could have believed to be, any where but in picture: and that which yet further increaft my wonder, was how they fhould come thus bare, having no turf upon them, or earth to produce one..........

Robert Plot's monumental study of the early history of Staffordshire is unique, for he only published one other similar county history - that of Oxfordshire, and since he was Keeper of the Ashmolean Museum and Professor of Chemistry at the University of Oxford, Staffordshire was greatly privileged to receive his investigative attentions. Plot addressed the work to King James the Second, and in his dedication he stated that he had the *'confidence to lay the like account of Stafordfhire at Your Majefties feet, and appeal once more to Your Roial Judgment; wherein if fuccesful, I shall little value what other men think; but cheerfully acquiefce in Your Majefties decifion, as in duty becomes'*. Plot was clearly a man who would stand by his word and opinions, come what may. A bit like yourself, perhaps, Nithsdale! The book retains the glorious language of the Seventeenth Century, and uses the letter 'f' as the letter 's', which makes it difficult to read but adds to its authenticity. The book is as much a work of literature as of history, and the author's poem on his 'Natural History of Staffordshire' concludes:

> With thy Victorious Charitable hand
> Point out the hidden Treafures of our Land.
> Envy or Ignorance do what they will
> Thou haft a bleffing from the Mufes Hill.
> Great be thy fpirit as thy Works divine,
> Shew thou thy Maker's Praife, We Poets will fing thine.

AS YOU CONTINUE along the hilly road to Buxton beyond Upperhulme you cannot fail to become aware of the dramatic change in the landscape.

Presently we found ourselves immediately beneath, and then running along side, the Ramshaw Rocks, with a view on our left across the top of the Roches, and a panorama of Leek in the distance behind. We noticed all manner of weird and fantastic shapes along the skyline of the Rocks, and readily realised we were in the Highlands of North Stafford.

As far as I am aware, my friend, you are the only person who has referred to the moorlands as the 'Highlands of Staffordshire,' but what a fitting title it is, and so typical of your pithy aphorisms. Today the brightly-coloured anoraks and ropes of climbers stand out in sharp contrast to the dark Millstone Grit of the rocks to which they cling like flies on a wall. The shouts of the instructors serve to remind you that the exhilarating sport of rock climbing has made a big impact on the Staffordshire Moorlands. The nursery slopes of the Roches have become the kindergarten for many who will later aspire to greater heights - perhaps the Alps, Andes or Himalayas. Many a famous personality in the mountaineering world has cut his first climbing teeth, perhaps literally, on the nursery slopes of the rugged Roches. These more unassuming moorland rocks boast climbing routes with such imposing names as the Great Chimney, Raven Rock Gully, Bengal Buttress and The Crippler. The rock faces of the Roches have been carved into fantastic shapes by the erosive action of countless centuries, jagged fingers grabbing at the stormy sky. Storm and tempest, winter gales, hail, ice and snow have achieved a result beyond the art and skill of any human sculptor, and the rocks stand bold against the skyline like some prehistoric monsters surveying the scene of their primeval battlefields. These dramatic rocks are seen at their best with a big, wild and stormy sky behind them, for they are not tame and gentle in any way.

Education of a more fundamental nature was provided for the children of the neighbourhood, growing up in the shadow of these rocks, by the tiny school at Ramshaw.

Ah, Playtime! I trow we all remember playtime. Those few

moments of sweetness sandwiched between hours of all manner
of elementary monotony, from multiplication to the intricacies
and irregularities of the verb 'to be'. The playtime which was
denied us at the approach of examinations, or when the teacher,
in his supreme autocracy, had arisen from the wrong side of the
bed. Life then was not all one grand sweet song; but what would
we not give for one short old-time playtime of innocent
amusement and reckless abandonment, even if it should end in
a swollen eye and an interview with the master. These sliding
wenches make me morose. Poor little hussies; ye know not what
woe the world is hoarding for ye!'

Woe indeed, my friend, for neither you nor they knew at the
time that within the next ten years the world would be torn apart by
the cataclysm of the First World War - a conflict which would touch
the lives of these children, perhaps the loss of father, brother or
sweetheart, just as it struck most families in the land. The declining
rural population and other economic factors forced the closure of the
school a number of years ago, and now the children who live in the
area go to the modern school at Blackshaw Moor or travel by bus into
Leek for their education.

IT HAS BEEN SAID that the bleak, treeless moorlands lack colour
and character, but this is not so. The changing seasons in their turn
clothe the moors in varied garb. Their dark and sombre winter coat,
whitened by deep snows and penetrating frost, lying thickly on leaf
and branch, for weeks on end, has a 'terrible beauty' all of its own.
The greening of the spring and the coming of summer introduces a
speckled blend of colours into the scene, with the various moorland
wild flowers, such as harebells, coltsfoot, eyebright, yarrow, thistle,
the ubiquitous heather and the sudden flash of bright yellow in the
little clumps of gorse. And now, with the lengthening days, the
landscape puts on another white coat, speckled this time by the soft-
tufted cotton grass gently nodding in the breeze - a sudden flash of
winter out of season. Early autumn sees the heather brilliantly
purple, and the bracken russet brown, springing to fiery life as it
catches the rays of the late sun. Then, as the days get shorter, all

turns black again, in the bare, windswept long winter.

The road, much like the one travelled by the highwayman in the poem by Alfred Noyes, himself a Staffordshire man, *'a river of moonlight over the purple moor'*, drives on past Morridge Top:

......a small triangular affair, a mile across the open moor- flanked road from Middle Hills, which, in addition to its three gaunt and bleak houses, embraces a small chapel, and has what you may call a nodding acquaintance with the neighbouring village of Flash.

TO REACH THE VILLAGE of Flash we take the sharp left-hand turn off the main road just before Flash Bar. Flash, at just over 1500 feet above sea level, has the reputation of being the highest village in England. The sturdy little cottages and houses are mostly built with local stone, so that they blend nicely with the landscape of which they are so much a part. There is a small church, hugging the hillside as if to shelter its former residents, who now lie quietly in the churchyard, from the bleak moorland winds, like a mother hen with her brood. Edward Bradbury, in his splendid Victorian guide book 'All about Derbyshire,' published in 1884, has a lovely word-picture of Flash Church:

> We alight to enter the Church, close by the roadside. It is not picturesque. It is a squat, ugly edifice. It has not even the saving merit of being considered old, and cannot, consequently, win the respect paid to age. A list of bygone benefactions are painted on the wall. The donors have long been dust, but their little liberalities remain.
>
> > The good that men do lives after them;
> > The evil is oft interred with their bones,'
>
> - if common consent will allow Mark Antony to stand corrected. The inscriptions on the lichen-stained gravestones are in some cases curious. These moorland men live long lives. The testimony of the tombs is that Death takes only the very old. The Clock of Life, when once started, goes the round of the Dial. The sexton can almost tell whose grave he will next dig. Death goes by seniority among these gray hills. One of the tombstones attracts us by its quaintness. On the tomb is the design of two coffins in stone. The inscription on the headstone tells us of one, Keziah, wife of Thomas Brunt. She died in child-bearing in November, 1813, in her thirty-third year. Then follows this verse, which is better than most graveyard literature:

'The boy's mother closes all her woes
In bringing forth a son with dying throes.
His cares are all to come : hers all are passed;
The son's first moments are the mother's last.
His life's her death; her death his life supplies;
He kills in birth, and she in bearing dies.'

Thomas Brunt, the husband, continued to walk these hills, enjoying roast beef and nut-brown ale, until 1864. When he joined his wife he was a patriarch of eighty-four. The majority of his neighbours have as long an 'innings.'

Flash, like most moorland villages, has a pub, the New Inn, and a large Methodist chapel, standing tall and proud, clearly visible across the fields from the main road nearly a mile away. The pub is still in business, and continues to welcome moorland travellers, but the chapel is not. It stands today as a memorial to its former glory days, before modern trends decimated the local population, retaining its outward appearance, it is now a listed building. Originally built in 1784, when John Wesley himself was tramping the land, it was largely rebuilt in 1821. The chapel had a large gallery, where musicians would play, and an enormous pulpit, both typical features of Methodist architecture, symbolic of the way the hymns would be sung lustily, and the Word preached vigorously, and often at great length. There is a strongly-held belief that Wesley himself actually preached there on one of his several visits to the area between 1772 and 1788. Its size belies its rural location, and it is difficult to imagine that in its heyday every pew would be filled by the farmers, miners and quarrymen of the area, with their families. Indeed, when the Leek Methodist Circuit was formed in 1793, it is recorded that Flash had more members than Leek.

A few years ago a familiar sight along the roads linking these moorland chapels was the visiting Methodist parson, travelling by Morris Minor, rather than horseback. Although he was stationed in Leek he loved to visit the country chapels in his care - his 'hill stations,' as he called them, having served as a missionary in India. He was a cricket fanatic, and when he retired from the full time ministry he took to umpiring in his local leagues. He said then that he wore his white robes on Saturday to dispense justice, and his black robes on Sunday to dispense grace!

Flash also gave its name to a novel published in 1928 by His Honour Judge Ruegg, a circuit judge at that time. The novel, now long out of print, enjoyed great success in its day, running into several editions, and has helped to perpetuate the romantic imagery of the area, which is singularly lacking in authentic literature.

I recall visiting Flash on the day that Sir Winston Churchill died, when I learned that a death had occurred in the village that same day. An old quarryman, well over eighty, who lived alone had been found dead in his cottage. It was a sobering thought - two men, one a famous statesman known throughout the world, and the other, a lonely old man, known to but a few of his isolated village neighbours, united in death, the great leveller. But now, my dear friend Nithsdale, we must return again to our route.....

TRAVELLING ON OUR WAY, we return to the main road and follow it round the sharp left-hand bend at Flash Bar. The name reminds us that in the days of the turnpike roads this was the site of a toll bar. We then turn left, following the sign to Knotbury.

We left our carriage in a bye-path and walked down a steep, stony cart track to Three Shire Heads, where the counties of Derby, Stafford and Chester are separated only by the confluence of the embryo Dane and a nameless moorland tributary. In this romantic home of the red grouse, surrounded by high heather-clad hills, and adorned with many a miniature canyon, the fugitive, swindling Flash-man was wont, in old times, to evade the law officers of one county by the simple process of moving into the next.

These wild moorland areas abound in legends and myths. The 'Flash-men' you referred to were no doubt the forgers of spurious coins, who, legend has it, found these remote spots ideal for their nefarious undercover activities - they could work undisturbed by the law and other inquisitive eyes. There are also stories of illegal sporting activities, such as cock-fighting, and even prize fights. One such story recounts that a fight had been arranged between two bare-knuckle prize fighters, the Burslem Bruiser and Preston Pat, to take place near the county borders. A certain magistrate, observing that the arranged site was within his county boundary, had the arena moved a few yards into the neighbouring county, which was outside his jurisdiction as a JP, and so he was able to enjoy the contest, and indulge in a little gambling on the side, with a clear conscience.

Three Shire Heads is a delectable spot. It can only be approached on foot - cars cannot reach it, and this adds to its charm, for it remains the domain of the walker. The ubiquitous motor-car has no place here. Its very remoteness protects it from the inevitable invasion of car-borne trippers, only wishing to park by the stream, deck chairs out, transistors blasting the peace of the place, and a desert of litter when they leave.

Here we are walking the old trade highways, for the area is interlaced with packhorse routes, and one can picture the old packmen, carriers, and jaggers of bygone days, transporting salt from Cheshire to the farms of Derbyshire, mohair, silk and cotton from the mills of Macclesfield and Lancashire, and goods of all kinds from industry to agriculture - yesterday's highways of commerce and trade. The splendid packhorse bridge at Panniers Pool (the name was recorded as early as 1533) has been widened at some stage of its history; its typical low parapets so constructed to allow the passage of heavily-laden mules. This was an important and much used section of the packhorse road network. William Morris, the Victorian artist, designer, writer and poet, and a leading figure in the Arts and Crafts movement, himself no stranger to the silk dying industry of Leek, has some apt words:

> Forget six counties overhung with smoke,
> Forget the snorting stream and piston stroke,
> Forget the spreading of the hideous town;
> Think rather of the packhorse on the down.
>
> (The Wanderers)

Like most places which have a magic all of their own, Three Shire Heads has something different to offer whatever the season of the year. In winter the heavy snow and deep, biting frost will transform the scene into a three-dimensional Christmas card more magical than any devised by man. In spring, after the snows have melted, or following a heavy rainstorm the infant River Dane becomes a raging torrent, roaring over the rocks - a precocious juvenile, bursting its own infantile strength, like Kipling's river in a

Packhorse route, near Three Shire Heads

far-away land, 'up an' brimmin.' Under the summer sun the gentler bubbling of the stream blends with the calls of the moorland birds to create an atmosphere of peace and calm, to ease the most troubled spirit. This is where you will hear the cuckoo in May and June, as I have done, when his distinctive call followed me all the way along the track below Turn Edge and the circuit of Cut-thorn Hill.

Three Shire Heads is a very special place in many ways, where technology and the twentieth century have made little impact. You return on foot, following the track below Turn Edge, which eventually becomes a narrow road overlooking the deep valley carved by a small stream. Some years ago I was walking along this road with a small group. The rain was pouring down, a heavy, soaking moorland rain, and along a narrow section the road was blocked by a broken down farm vehicle standing plumb in the middle of the road, leaning towards the drop at a perilous angle, with one of its rear wheels off. As we approached a wet and bedraggled oil-stained body hauled itself from underneath the vehicle, and said with a grin, "Are you enjoying your walk?" We asked if we could give him a push, to get the vehicle off the road, and he said, still grinning, "Nay, lads, it's no use. Yo wunna shift 'er, 'er's buggered!" Then, with a smile as wide as the moorlands, he said, "I think I'm going to be here for a long time yet. I shall be late for tea today!" What stoical fortitude these hardy Moorlanders possess! Poor chap, that breakdown was probably not the worst thing that had happened to him that day!

The *'tumble-down, often one-chimneyed houses of ancient colliers,'* which you refer to, WH, once moorland farms and smallholdings, have now, in many instances, become weekend homes or holiday cottages. The itinerant population of the Staffordshire Moorlands now fluctuates from season to season - and even from weekend to weekend - for a new industry, tourism, has come to the moorlands since you first travelled these highways.

RETURNING TO THE MAIN ROAD, we soon pass from Staffordshire into Derbyshire. Over the wall on the right, and a few yards down the field, is Dove Head, the modest source of the River Dove, marked by a stone bearing the intertwined initials, I.W. and

C.C. - perpetuating the memory of Isaac Walton and Charles Cotton, to whom the Dove, in its lower reaches below Hartington, became their piscatorial paradise - more of these two gentlemen later.

The main road climbs steadily towards Axe Edge and on to Buxton, famed spa town, which came into prominence as a health resort in Victorian times, observed by Edward Bradbury in the following terms:.....

> the most interesting natural phenomena at Buxton are the thermal springs, which have been in repute for their healing qualities since the times of the Romans, and which have made the Spa of the Peak the English Wildbad.

Buxton, dear Nithsdale, you described in your typical observant terms, as a *'city of hydros, hotels, baths, bath-chairs, gout, rheumatism, consumption, and all manner of other things peculiar to sanatoria.'* You must have felt some affection for Buxton, for, as if to redress the balance, lest your observations should be deemed disparaging, you finally referred to Buxton as *'a really delightful town.'*

Leaving Buxton we follow your route along the road to the Cat and Fiddle, an exposed highway over the open moors...

> *an unfenced moorland road towards the 'Cat and Fiddle', which is famous as being one of the highest public-houses in England. We could see this place, when we turned into the Congleton Road, from a mile and a half below .... the wooden posts we observed by the road-side were to guide travellers when the country was covered deep in snow in winter.*

The Cat and Fiddle ('Fidelle') and the wild moorland surrounding it inspired Edward Bradbury to pen one of his splendid word pictures. These old Victorian writers of guide books certainly knew a thing or two about writing vivid descriptive passages.

> This lonely hostelry among the hills stands low-spreading and four-square against the winds. No wider or wilder moors could surround a human dwelling. Hills rise above hills; rocks oppose rocks; moors mingle in moors. There are valleys within valleys: hollows hide hollows. The prevailing tint is gray; but in the conflagration of a stormy sunset there is a study of intense tints - a spread of fiery splendour - that the boldest artist would hesitate to attempt .... to those who love a moorland wilderness of gritstone, heath, peat, moss, miry bog and inky rill, this mountain waste has ineffable charms.

A story about the origin of the old inn sign tells that a certain Duke of Devonshire who enjoyed his visits to the inn, had a picture made of his favourite cat and fiddle which he presented to the landlord as a token of his gratitude for many convivial visits. Dr Brewer, in his 'Phrase and Fable,' suggests that the name is a corruption of 'Caton Fidele,' that is 'Caton the Faithful' sometime governor of Calais. He also suggests a much more obvious meaning, simply the old game of 'cat,' or trap-ball, and a fiddle for dancing provided for the customers.

You travelled this high moorland road, Nithsdale, and ....
For several miles we journeyed across a beautiful heath, with the Upper Dane Valley on our left, passing Dane Bower quarries. We were now among the Cheshire Highlands, in country which was in striking contrast to the level land which is usually associated with the name, Cheshire. Presently we saw the locality of Three Shire Heads, hidden by the surrounding uplands about three-quarters of a mile away; and a mile beyond, on our right, the highland village of Wildboarclough, high upon the hill-side, and over-topped by the conical peak of Shuttlingslow. Our next village was the small, but exquisitely picturesque, Allgreave. Another mile, by winding, steep, and in places very narrow roads, brought us to Wincle, whence we quickly travelled to Danebridge.

THE DANE VALLEY, a well-wooded river valley, verdant and green, in contrast to the wild and treeless moorland above, we approach through the old village of Wincle. The largely Victorian church and old school at Wincle are reminders of a bygone age, when there were many more people in the area. Depopulation of rural areas is a twentieth century trend, which has had a considerable effect on the Staffordshire Moorlands. 'Here doe O Lord sure plant thy Word', say the words in stone over the church door. It is said that the minister here had no fixed stipend, the people paying 'what they pleased for preaching, when there was any.' The sowing of the Word was clearly haphazard, and the subsequent harvest probably even more so. Indeed, there is a story that the parish clerk, in the absence of a clergyman, once conducted the funeral of a child. He looked out in vain for the parson, the mourners were getting impatient, the sun was setting, so he "just slipped on the surplice" and conducted the burial service, justifying his action by saying that 'after all, it was but a little 'un.'

FOLLOWING YOUR ROUTE, Nithsdale, as we begin to descend through Wincle, the beautiful Dane Valley reveals itself. Approaching Danebridge down the steep hill we pass the 'Ship Inn' on the left. The old inn sign depicts the vessel 'Nimrod', a reminder of a great adventure undertaken by a member of the Brocklehurst family, of nearby Swythamley Hall, who travelled with Sir Ernest Shackleton to the Antarctic in 1908. As a means of raising money to fund his expedition, Shackleton took on a number of paying members, and Brocklehurst paid to join the 'Nimrod' on its journey south. It seems a far cry from this lovely green valley to the frozen wastes of Antarctica but memories of home would no doubt sustain him in those bitter, testing conditions. Had he, one wonders, since he was a contemporary of yours, read your exquisite description of Danebridge?

Danebridge is a beautiful, half-Cheshire, half-Stafford, hamlet, on the Dane. The bridge across the river is its main feature, and we thoroughly enjoyed the evening prospect up and down the magnificent valley; and, as we looked down I fancied an old road leading to a ford across the river below, and recognised the usefulness of the bridge. There are several steel-rope bridges in the vicinity which are used by local people today. ...... After tea in the open air we crossed into Staffordshire, and climbed the opposite bank to Swythamley Park. The driver favoured a shady avenue on the left, but we would go down a steep incline to Bearda. We found this an exquisite little hollow, with a small mill and a lot of water.

In bygone days there was some industry in the Danebridge area. There were several watermills on the Dane or its tributaries. William Yates' map of Staffordshire, dated 1775, shows a colour mill at Danebridge and a paper mill at Gig Hall, as well as a corn mill and a saw mill at Bearda, but these old mills have all disappeared, the gentle clacking of their water wheels silenced.

BEFORE LEAVING DANEBRIDGE we must pause to recall a dark incident from the area's past - the sad story of young John Naden, a tale of illicit love and murder. In 1731 a young man named John Naden was employed as a hired servant to Robert Brough, a farmer, of White Lea. Brough would often be away at markets during the day, leaving his young wife at home. The situation where wife and servant were left alone together at the isolated farm led to its inevitable consequences, young Naden fell victim to readily available charms. Mrs Brough developed an obsessive desire for Naden - a desire so powerful that she urged Naden to murder her husband, promising that he would be rewarded by her continuing love, and possession of the farm, as its new master. A story as old as time, Naden fell victim to the fatal charms of his mistress. He made one unsuccessful attempt at murdering his master on his way home from Congleton market, earning the reproof of Mrs Brough. She urged him to try again. Some time later, Naden followed Brough home from Leek market, and along the quiet stretch of road near the Abbey Inn he cut his master's throat. When the murder was discovered Mrs Brough incited Naden to say that he had witnessed the murder taking place, and that the killer was an innocent neighbour, William Wardle. Just how the true facts were discovered is not fully known. It is said that Naden made one fatal mistake - he left his knife at the scene of the crime. Furthermore, a number of persons spoke on Wardle's behalf, confirming his innocence, and Wardle was acquitted as not guilty.

On August 25th 1731 Naden confessed to the murder, admitting that the allurement of his mistress had led him to commit the deed. He was tried for murder, found guilty and sentenced 'that on Tuesday, the 31st August, he should be brought to his master's door ..... and there hanged till he was dead, and afterwards conveyed to Gun Common, near Danebridge, and there hanged in chains.' This sad story of the last man to hang in the Leek area is now part of our local folklore, and according to the account in Miller's 'Olde Leeke', it provoked much public interest. The local inns were crowded on the day of the hanging, and church choirs turned out to sing a funeral hymn. Miller quotes 'The Grub Street Journal' of September, 16th, 1731:

Stafford, August 30. This day John Naden who murdered his master, Mr

Brough, was carried on a horse having his legs ty'd and hand cuft, to Leek. The
next morning he was carried to the highest hill on Gun Heath, within a quarter
of a mile of his master's house, where in the presence of some thousands of
spectators he confessed the facts for which he died. The gibbet is 21 feet high,
and may be seen 5 miles round the country. The chains which were made by
one of Birmingham, are made in so curious a manner, that they will keep his
bones together till they turn to powder, if the iron will not last long.

A gruesome end indeed! And Mrs Brough? According to the
traditions of Naden listed by Miller, she 'died a truly wretched death
at either Peck's House, or Cloud House, in Rushton.'

AT ONE TIME it was necessary to obtain a permit from the Squire
of Swythamley if you wished to explore the splendid walking country
around Back Forest, between Danebridge and Gradbach. Today,
fortunately, a network of public paths and access paths now allows
the walker reasonable entry to all parts of this delightful area, rich in
all aspects of moorland natural history. Curlew and kestrel wheel
overhead, and the red grouse can often be seen or heard. Just beyond
the road bridge, as we begin to climb out of the valley, in a quiet
retreat, off the road to the right, stands Danebridge Methodist
Chapel. Like most of these sturdy and unpretentious moorland
chapels, it was strongly supported in its early days by the farming
and mill-working families in the district. Built in 1834, its support
was sufficiently strong to allow a gallery to be added in 1850. In
1903 a major reconstruction took place, when it was remodelled by
George Clarke, a Lincolnshire man, who was agent to Sir Philip
Brocklehurst.

Two more church buildings have some points of interest, as we
follow the road back towards Leek. First, the former estate church of
Swythamley, now converted to a dwelling. Built by the Brocklehursts
in 1905, the church had two unique features - a fine rose window,
usually found in much larger churches or cathedrals, and a water-
powered peal of bells, the mechanics of which were very intricate.
Then, at Gun End, on the sharp right-hand bend in the road, the
Methodist Chapel is also now a house. It is said that this was literally
'bought for a song', the Squire of Swythamley having promised to

give a small plot of land on which a chapel could be built if the people would sing a favourite hymn for him at Swythamley Hall.

And so we travel on, passing Eleven Lane Ends (count them carefully, and you will see that there are indeed eleven!), to join the main Macclesfield road back towards Leek. At the end of our first outing together, you, dear Nithsdale, can have the final word.

The scenery all along was exquisite, and, after passing through a small wood, we turned down-hill into the Macclesfield and Leek Road, observing Rudyard Hall on our left. N. told us Rudyard Lake and Rudyard lay immediately on our right, but we saw nothing of them today. Pool End and Highfield were pointed out to us; and presently we crossed the Churnet into Leek, driving up the steep Mill Street into the town, and making our first acquaintance with the stately church, the spacious Market Place and Derby Street in the gathering gloom.

Doxey's Pool.

Old Limekilns, Froghall

CHAPTER II

AN AFTERNOON OUTING
Leekbrook, Basford, Ipstones, Froghall, Kingsley,
Wetley Rocks and Cheddleton

RAIN IS A FEATURE of the climate of the Staffordshire Moorlands. When you first undertook this trip, Nithsdale, the weather was somewhat unsettled, and determined to try out a range of transport, you chose a governess car, now rarely seen. You, with your friend Wilkinson and his daughter Jessie all packed inside and *'had a smart little pony, which stepped out quite briskly.'* We will travel by motor car, for we have many miles to travel, and much to see before dark.

Leaving Leek, we turn left at the end of Southbank Street into the Cheadle Road. On this corner stands the splendid All Saints Church, which demands our attention before we leave town. Built in 1885-7 to the design of the famous and influential Victorian architect, Richard Norman Shaw, the church has a spacious interior with a low clerestory. Its rather squat central tower has a unique appeal. The land on which the church stands was given partly by John Challinor, whose brother Joseph also gave £3500 towards the cost of the building. The Challinors were an important Leek family of lawyers. Another influential benefactor was the silk manufacturer Hugh Sleigh, who owned property in St Edward Street, where he commissioned Norman Shaw also to design the Tudor-style Spout Hall - Victorian architecture at its best. The building of the church was undertaken by a local builder, James Heath of Endon, and his work greatly impressed Norman Shaw with its quality and high standard - an accolade indeed from such an eminent person. Heath kept a detailed diary of his building work, and his entry for the Consecration Day of the church in July 1887 is both interesting and amusing:

> The masons are not working today because I gave them a half day's holiday to enable them to go to the service. They have got on the beer and are not now at work; dreadful, isn't it?

All Saints Church has many interesting features. The chancel painting and panelling is by Gerald Horsley. The Gothic style pulpit and the reredos are attributed to Lethaby, and some of the stained glass is by Morris and Co. There are a number of examples of the work of the Leek School of Needlework, the enterprise, encouraged by William Morris, of Mrs Wardle and her circle of friends who meticulously produced fine examples of the skill of the needlewoman. The concentration of so much superb Victorian architecture, art and design in one church moved the late Poet Laureate, Sir John Betjeman to comment:

> On this church subsequent artists in Leek have given their best stained glass, embroidery, textiles and paintings, so that its uplifting spaciousness under that severely simple roof is one of the wonders of England. Neither words nor photographs can really do justice to great architecture such as you see at All Saints. The only way to appreciate the thought and affection which have been lavished on it is to remain in it and look; best of all to use the building for what it was designed - worship.

On the opposite corner of the road stands the old Compton School, designed by Robert Edgar and built in 1863. Its ecclesiastical features are a reminder that it served as a church before All Saints was built, when it was under the pastoral care of the curate from St Luke's. When All Saints Church was opened it became a church school. Notice the splendid relief figures in the wall, symbolising the highly-held Victorian virtues of learning and diligence in study.

The 1880s, golden years of Leek's prosperity, saw a great upsurge in church building in the town. The old Parish Church of St Edward the Confessor engaged another eminent Victorian architect, George Edmund Street, to design a new chancel. The Methodists were expanding their work, and the Roman Catholics, just down the road, in nearby Compton, were building the new St Mary's Church, at the same time as All Saints. Its architect was Albert Vicars, and it was supported by the generosity of Henry Bermingham and his family, devout Roman Catholics, who lived at nearby Ladydale, and owned the large silk factory opposite. The church is high and lofty, an impression best gained from the approach via St Edward Street, where it dominates the scene ahead. The building of the church, with its lofty spire, must have been a spectacular sight in Victorian Leek.

We can imagine the local folk raising their eyes in wonder to watch the erection of the large cross on top of the tall spire - it would be a fine sight, and a splendid feat of engineering, for the cross is huge!

BUT WE RETURN TO OUR JOURNEY, to follow the Cheadle Road out of town, as you describe, my friend ....

We drove down a deep cutting, below some pretty alms-houses standing by the road-side to the cemetery, and then through an open country with an extensive view on the right and woodland high on the slope on the left.

The alms houses which you mentioned are the Condlyffe Alms Houses, built in 1882 at a cost of about £4000. Alms houses were usually built on the generosity of some former landowner, manufacturer or local gentry. Miss Elizabeth Condlyffe was the last surviving member of a prosperous local family who lived in Derby Street. This site was given, and a farm at Upperhulme, for the endowment of the charity established in their name. According to Miller's 'Olde Leeke' these alms houses were also designed by Norman Shaw, and having in mind Miss Condlyffe's strong involvement with All Saints Church, this is quite likely. There are other alms houses in Leek, notably, perhaps, the Ash Alms Houses nearby, at the bottom of Compton. These are the oldest in the town, being founded 13 March 1676, by Elizabeth Ash, daughter of William Jolliffe, a wealthy silk mercer, who lived at Leek Old Hall (later the Red Lion Hotel) in the Market Place. They were to accommodate eight poor women, widows or spinsters, being nominated from the parishes of Leek, Endon, Leekfrith and Bradnop and Onecote. Inmates had to be sober and well-behaved, and a regular communicant at church. No gossips, scandal-mongers or drunkards were allowed, and the ladies were not permitted to have anyone living with them, except, if necessary, a nurse. There was a clothing allowance of a purple gown at Christmas. In spite of these stringent conditions, which would no doubt exclude certain ladies of Leek, the alms houses have never lacked residents, and continue so today. In Fountain Street are the Carr Alms Houses, a Victorian establishment, erected in 1892 at a cost of £4000. They were endowed by Miss Isabella Carr in memory of her sisters Ellen and

Roseanne Carr, her wealth having been gained from the family silk manufacturing business.

There is no reason to believe that the altruism and charity of the benefactors was anything but genuine, and they stand today as an reminder of the affluence which existed in Leek in former days. Whilst it is true that the pioneers of the local silk industry made their fortunes out of the town, they also left a rich legacy of fine Victorian buildings and generous endowments for the benefit of succeeding generations in the town.

The changing face of capitalism and finance is brought home to the traveller following your route out of Leek, Nithsdale, where your *'extensive view on the right'* is now dominated by the huge new building society offices. The millions of pounds invested therein, and the vast sums which flit across the computer screens each day, make the wealth of our forbears seem puny indeed!

It may seem strange, Nithsdale, but this part of the town was largely unexplored and unknown to us as lads. Perhaps it was a bit too 'posh', or maybe it was the nearness of the cemetery that deterred us, but on the odd occasions we did come this way it was usually to walk through Ballington Wood. Ballington Wood had all the essential ingredients for an exciting excursion - a brook, a wood and mud! Brooks were always interesting, and demanded further attention. You never knew what you would find in a brook. Too shallow for fish, there would always be lots of other forms of microscopic life, as well as tadpoles and frogs. And if you were really lucky you might get a good bag of watercress, which would stand you in good stead with the folks at home - unless, of course, it happened to be pondweed, then you were really in trouble! Woods were always magical, entrancing places, and Ballington Wood and birdnesting (or 'brid-naysing', as older local folk called it) went hand-in-hand, but always in the true cause of science, you understand - we were just amateur naturalists, pursuing a legitimate interest. However, a few lines by the poet JM Synge will serve as a mild rebuke:

> You great-great-grandchildren
> Of birds I've listened to
> I think I robbed your ancestors
> When I was young as you.

When you followed the path through the wood, and climbed the fields beyond, you reached a place where you would find the muddiest mud in the area. The path by Cowhay Farm was always gloriously muddy, thick mud which seeped over the top of your boots and squelched around your toes, so that the walk back home via Lowe Hill Bridge and down the Ashbourne Road was done with the scars of battle on your feet and clinging to your boots!

BIRCHALL PLAYING FIELD is a great asset to Leek, for it has played host to many sports - rugby, football, cricket, athletics - good facilities for youth teams and organisations who would otherwise have nowhere to play. The 'Lads and Dads' football matches on Sunday mornings are supported by crowds of proud parents, with several games being played at the same time on the broad acres. Once a year, however, Birchall is transformed, when the country puts on its best suit and comes to town for the annual Leek Agricultural Show. We must visit this venue again, Nithsdale, for it is a splendid event, and a fine example of a traditional rural show - and you will be able to see what has changed and what remains from your day.

There is still the showing of cattle, horses and other farm livestock, finely groomed as if from some bovine beauty parlour. The farmer, or his daughter or son, wear a smart white smock to parade their prize beasts proudly around the show ring, and a highly-charged competitive air pervades the whole event. More modern attractions have also been introduced for the huge crowds which flock to Birchall on this one Saturday in July, for the show is now very much a town and country affair. Hence we are likely to see police motor cyclists rubbing shoulders with shire horses, medieval jousters following show jumpers into the arena, prize cattle giving way to circus performers, and candy floss and hot-dogs competing with the traditional Womens' Institute fare of cream scones and fruit cakes. All aspects of life in the Moorlands focus themselves on Birchall Playing Field on this great day of the Leek Show!

THE LEEKBROOK AREA has experienced many changes since your day, Nithsdale. Just before the old railway bridge here, there used to be a toll house in the days of the turnpike road, but this has long disappeared. The railway, too, has gone, and a new industrial estate has been established, straddling the road as you pass under the bridge, its modern factory units looking somewhat incongruous in this rural setting. There is an unusual war memorial on the left, in the form of a plain flagpole mounted in rough-hewn rock, with a memorial tablet recording the names of the young men from the area who lost their lives in that war which ripped Europe apart soon after the years you were in Leek.

Leekbrook Junction, in the days of the North Staffordshire Railway - the old "Knotty" - was a very busy place. A junction in the literal sense of the word, it stood at the intersection of lines running north to Leek and Macclesfield, south through Cheddleton and the scenic Churnet Valley to Uttoxeter, west through Endon and Milton to Stoke and the industrial Potteries and east to Ipstones, Waterhouses and the Cauldon Lowe Quarries. There were three signal boxes: Leekbrook East, North and South, and the Leekbrook station platform stood on the curve of the Stoke line. To the north, there was a locomotive shed and water tower, and possibly the tallest signal on the entire "Knotty" system. An electric tramway served the nearby Cheddleton Mental Hospital from a special hospital platform near to Leekbrook South signalbox. It is a sobering thought that the national railway system, developed in the mid-19th century, which was at its height in your time, Nithsdale, has now been largely consigned to the realms of industrial archaeology and nostalgia.

Leekbrook has long been associated with silk dyeing, and synonymous with this is the name of Joshua Wardle. The factory which bears his name still stands, another reminder of the area's industrial past. He was the father of Thomas Wardle, who was born in that other silk town of Macclesfield in 1831, educated at Leek Grammar School and married Elizabeth, daughter of Hugh Wardle of Leek. Thomas Wardle was deeply involved in the burgeoning silk industry locally, nationally and internationally, serving on many major committees, and organising exhibitions and conferences. He was President of the Society of Dyers and Colourists, and in your time, Nithsdale, in 1906, he presented an address at the 50th anniversary celebrating the discovery of mauve and the foundation of the coal-tar colour industry by Sir W. H. Perkin in 1856, which revolutionised the silk dyeing trade. Thomas Wardle travelled the world widely, and he recommended to the Government of India that sericulture, the breeding of silk-worms, should be promoted in Kashmir, which had an excellent climate for the growth of mulberry trees. In 1898 the Maharajah of Kashmir instructed him to spend £1500 on European silk-worm eggs, this amount being doubled the following year. He received a Knighthood for his services to the silk industry in 1897, and was also a Fellow of the Chemical and Geological Societies. He wrote a number of scientific and technical books, mainly on the subjects of silk or geology, amongst which are: 'The Geology of the Neighbourhood of Leek', 'Silk Power-loom Weaving in France', 'The Dyes and Tans of India', 'On Tussar Silk' and 'The Wild Silks of India'.

A notable feature of Thomas Wardle's life was his productive but often stormy association with William Morris, who made several visits to Leek between 1875 and 1877 in his quest for perfect colours for his printed fabrics. At that time Thomas Wardle's dye works were at Hencroft, on Abbey Green Road in Leek. Here, Morris would roll up his sleeves and work in the dye vats as he strove to find the ideal colours.

Sir Thomas had a fine country house at Swainsley, near Butterton, in the heart of the Manifold Valley, and his town house was in St Edward Street.

LEAVING THE BUSY MAIN ROAD at Leekbrook, my friend, we follow again your *'beautiful and shady lanes'* through Basford to Belmont Pools, being mindful that these narrow roads were built more for your era of transport than ours. The area around Belmont Pools is a delectable spot which you describe as a vista of *'exquisite reeded pools'* and *'sylvan loveliness'* - it is indeed. And what an apt name for such a beautiful place - Belmont literally 'a fair mountain', and even though there are no mountains here, its leafy, shaded pools make it a place of great beauty.

Beyond Belmont, on the road towards Ipstones, is the interesting Chapel House, nestling cosily amongst the trees on the right hand side of the road. It is a well-held belief, recorded by Rev.F.Brighton in his 'Tale of Ipstones', that the Chapel House was built by John Sneyd of the nearby Belmont Hall because of a dispute he had with the then Vicar of Ipstones, and that he installed a priest of his choice. How the dispute was resolved is not certain, but the chapel was never licensed for public worship, and became a private dwelling, whilst retaining its distinct ecclesiastical features.

LEAVING THE PEACE OF BELMONT, we travel on to the large village of Ipstones, or 'Appy Ippy', as it is somewhat endearingly called locally - one of the larger villages in the Staffordshire Moorlands area, but one which has a long and fascinating history. The name of the village has provided a puzzle for students of the origin of place-names. The 'stones' part is fairly clear, but the first syllable 'Ip' is the problem. Rev.F.Brighton, a former Vicar of Ipstones, points out that Loxdale, a historian of some antiquity, mentions the spelling 'Yppenstones' in the year 1220, and proceeds to say that 'the word Hyppestan is used in deeds dating 1209-1228'. He goes on to say that *'in the year 1228 William-de-Ipperstones, with ten others, is mentioned in a dispute in the reign of Edward I'*, and that the earliest record of the present-day spelling was in 1393, when John-de-Ipstones is mentioned. The ancient spelling 'YPPE' appears to mean an upper or elevated stone, which could refer to the high rocks above Sharpcliffe, and imply a strategic look-out position.

Ipstones is rather a large village, too compact to be purely agricultural. Half-a-dozen black-faced pitmen coming up the road solved the mystery; and yet the pits are several miles away. It is remarkable what distances colliers travel in going to their work.

You saw Ipstones as a mining village, WH, perhaps evocative of the Scottish mining communities of your youth. In the nineteenth century a rich seam of coal was discovered, about 2 feet 6 inches thick and known as the Crabtree seam, and this, together with many other small-scale coal and ironstone mining activities in the district between Ipstones, Kingsley and Cheadle, provided labour for the men of the area, as an alternative to the traditional industry of farming.

Ipstones has seen many changes since you first came this way. One of the larger moorland villages, its population has increased greatly since the Second World War, and modern housing developments stand alongside sturdy and substantial older properties. A great incursion of town into country occurred in the post-war years, when the demand for housing was met by the development of neat and tidy housing estates, many with the limits of the properties defined by the privet hedge. Allow me to digress for a few moments, whilst I tell you a story from my youth - the tale of Poobah's privet hedge. In the area where we lived, a certain man was the scourge of small boys in the neighbourhood, a self-styled lord of the avenue. We gave him the Gilbertian name of Poobah - 'the Lord High Everything Else'. Now Poobah had a fine, thick privet hedge of which he was very proud. However, we boys, being of an enquiring turn of mind, made an interesting discovery of a feature peculiar to privet hedges. We found that, if you give the leaves a sharp pluck about three inches from the end of the stalk, the end comes away, leaving about half an inch of an inner stalk protruding, with an equivalent hollow section in the end you have pulled away. With a little care, you can re-assemble the leaves by bringing the two parts together in a kind of 'spear and sheath' arrangement. Having made this discovery we decided to put it into to the test in an experiment at the expense of old Poobah. We spent an entire afternoon systematically dismantling his hedge and re-assembling it in the way I have described. Of course, deprived of their life-line, the ends quickly wilted and grew limp. Imagine the consternation and puzzlement of Poobah when he discovered his wilting hedge! We observed him from a safe distance, as his amazement turned to anger!

I digress again, my friend; so back to Ipstones, where I am sure the children are much better behaved! In spite of the many changes, Ipstones has managed to retain much of its essential character, particularly in the old centre of the village, around the old school, the pub and the post office, and Stocks Green, near the church.

The grey stone church of St Leonard built around 1790, has a later chancel by Gerald Horsley (1902), and contains memorials to the Sneyd family, whose influence on the area was extensive. Not only were they influential landowners, exercising a temporal authority, but the Rev. John Sneyd was the spiritual overseer of the parish from 1833 to 1861 - the archetypal nineteenth century squire/parson.

Let us visit the churchyard to find an interesting and unusual grave. Here, amongst the sturdy headstones, many of them several inches thick, is the last resting place of a local man who had declared that if there was a life after death his tomb would be broken asunder. A solid table tomb was erected to his memory, and today we can see that a mature tree has grown on the very spot, its solid trunk having completely shattered the stonework of the tomb! No hand of man, vandal or graverobber, has caused this damage - the tree speaks its own silent message.

Any village of the size of Ipstones needs a meeting place in addition to church, chapel, school and pub, and Ipstones got its Memorial Hall some years after your visit here. Since 1929 this spacious hall has provided a social centre for village activities with the adjoining Recreation Ground a safe play area for village youngsters. The money for the building was raised by public subscription, drawing heavily on the generosity of Mrs Boucher and the organising skills of Leo Lowndes. 'Mr. Ipstones' would have been an appropriate title for Leo Lowndes, for he was one of those village 'characters' who were the backbone of rural England. A veteran of the First World War, he came to Ipstones as the village schoolmaster and became involved with sports activities and parish affairs. A man of wit and humour, he knew everyone and was known by all, and his personality enabled him to bring together the talents and abilities of the people in making the dream of a village hall a reality.

Myths, legends and folklore abound in the Ipstones area. Stories of fairies and changelings are not uncommon, and one such tale is set at Bradshaw Farm, where a young mother took her baby out into the fields and laid down the child on a pile of hay whilst she went to help with the haymaking. At the end of the day she was astonished to discover that a fairy child had been exchanged for her own baby. She looked after the child as if it were her own, but it was rather a lower-class fairy. Nevertheless, the fairy child brought good luck to the woman. Money and other good things seemed to appear when needed, but when the child died a few years later, the bounty ceased. It would appear that even some fairies are mortal!

As might be expected, there are also stories of witches. A woman went to the local miller for a bag of flour. On her way home she met a witch, who asked what was in the bag she was carrying. She said that it was flour, but the witch denied this, and changed it into manure. On returning home, the woman left the bag in the cowshed. Later, her husband asked why she had left a bag of flour in this rather odd place. She said that it was not flour but manure, but her husband insisted that he had seen flour spilling out of the bag! This was indeed the case, for the manure had been changed back to flour.

The tradition of the Wandering Jew also has an Ipstones connection. Around the year 1850 the Jew called on a lame old man, and asked for a drink of beer. The old man agreed, but asked the Jew to draw his own, as he was lame. The stranger said he could cure the old man's lameness. "Take two or three balm leaves with your beer and you will be cured; but serve God constantly." The old man followed these instructions, and his lameness was cured. An old family herbal tells us that balm *possesses high stimulant and carminative properties, which render it valuable as a remedial agent. Balm is a good tonic, which strengthens the stomach, braces the nerves and elevates the mind by its exhilarating virtues. This valuable medicine should always be kept in the house........* It might be said that these properties also apply to the beer, but which of the two effected the old man's cure?

There are a number of fine houses in the Ipstones area. In their day, the gentry and the yeoman farmers locally built well for themselves, and have left several splendid examples of early vernacular architecture. Whitehough is a very ancient site indeed, and is a mixture of many different styles and periods. There was a medieval house on the site, but the present building dates mainly from the 17th century, so we have a heady mix of mullioned windows and Tudor chimneys, with a fine gazebo nearby. In the 17th century, Whitehough was owned by the Mellor family, who were devout Quakers. Other significant 17th century properties in the area are Sharpcliffe Hall and Moss Lee Hall, whilst Belmont Hall, well hidden from the road, overlooking the Churnet Valley, was a Sneyd family home for many years in the 19th century. It is clear that the

Ipstones area has had an abundance of affluent residents in bygone days.

WE LEAVE IPSTONES to travel on to Froghall and we descend the steep, winding road into the Churnet Valley. But how the industrial scene has changed as we reach the valley. No longer are there those..........

tremendous smoking chimneys, lime kilns, brick works, and the large buildings of the copper smelting works.

Your view of Froghall, dear friend, recalled its heyday as a major centre of industrialisation at the very heart of the Churnet Valley.

We found Froghall a most interesting place. We put up the horse and walked over the canal wharf, where tons and tons of limestone are brought from the quarries at Cauldon Lowe by a mineral railway, and either burned in the kilns here, or shipped in long and - except for their gaudy colouring - torpedo-boat-destroyer-like barges, for use in the blast furnaces of South Staffordshire and the Black Country. It was an animated scene and we enjoyed it thoroughly.........

Today it is difficult to imagine the industrialised scene which greeted you and your friends, for nature has reasserted itself at Froghall Basin. But there are many reminders. The huge bank of limekilns, which once belched their fumes and smoke to the heavens like a scene from Hades, are well-preserved, an important industrial archaeology site. The weather-beaten wharf-side warehouse, once the commercial nerve-centre, as goods and traffic passed along the canal, has been restored. The car-park and picnic site once resounded to the clang and rattle of the railway wagons, loaded with limestone from the quarries, descending the incline from Cauldon Lowe. The bank sides, once piled high with freshly-quarried limestone, awaiting shipment to the Potteries, or burning in the kilns, are now once more the habitat of a wide variety of flora and fauna. The gently lapping waters of the canal, which once surged and churned as the boats were loaded by gangs of sweating labourers, are now disturbed only by the mallard. And over the entire area there hung, like the breath of hell itself, a heavy pall of smoke, fumes and dust - a veritable Moorlands Inferno!

Today, in this now-tranquil spot, we can safely approach these limekilns - something which, in your day, Nithsdale, you may well have hesitated to do. Now the hungry mouths are still, the hearths are cold and they stand as an interesting relic. If we look closely at the surface of the massive dressed stone blocks and buttresses we see a series of neatly-cut patterns, here a diamond or a cross, there a star or an arrow. These are masons' marks, used by the stonemason to personalise his work, each mason having his own mark. These huge blocks of stone, quarried from the earth, laid down during countless centuries of geological time, bear the fossilised and fragmented remains of long-lost forms of life from before the time of man. And now, finally, man, with skilful human hands, has carved his own mark into these ancient rocks - a lesson, perhaps, on the continuity of time and creation, and man's place in the scheme of things.

But let us now cast our minds back a little over two hundred years, Nithsdale, to the time when the Caldon Canal was constructed. This is the canal which the demands of industry necessitated, for limestone was consumed in great quantities by the pottery kilns and blast furnaces. This is the canal which put an end to the prodigiously creative career of James Brindley, coughing his life away after catching one of those notorious Moorland chills whilst surveying the route. This is the canal which harnessed the skills of engineers like John Rennie in the construction of the tramway systems to bring the limestone from the quarries at Cauldon Lowe to the canal basin at Froghall, ready for transportation to the heart of the Potteries. This is the canal which had its life terminated by the coming of the railway in 1849, when the greater speed and carrying capacity of the iron monsters breathing steam made the slow canal boats redundant. And now the railway, which you commented upon, Nithsdale, has gone too, and the canal has come back to life - albeit with pleasure craft! History surely seems to work in cycles.

The Caldon Canal, opened in 1777, was constructed to convey limestone to Etruria in the Potteries, some 13$\frac{1}{2}$ miles away, at the junction with the Trent and Mersey Canal. But the quarries at Cauldon Lowe were a further four miles to the east, and a rise of 700 feet in land height. Because of this it was impossible to take the canal to the source of the limestone; Froghall, at the level of the River Churnet, was the nearest point. It was therefore necessary to construct industrial railways, or tramways, to transport the stone from the quarries to the canal basin at Froghall, and over the next 150 years or so there were three different systems, each one an improvement on its predecessor. The earliest line - a very rudimentary affair - was laid in haste in the late 1770s, and followed the valley of the Shirley Brook, where frost caused troubles for this primitive railway. A vivid description of this line appeared in 'The Coal Viewer and Engine Builder's Practical Companion' (1797) by John Curr of Sheffield - one of those quaintly surreal late 18th century accounts of early industry:

At Froghall in Staffordshire, they had a land conveyance for their limestone, which is three of four miles in length, one half of which is flat ground, and the other half, about two and a half or three inches descent in the yard; these roads, which are on the plan of what is called Newcastle waggon roads, are laid in a firm manner upon wood, (after having been at a great expence of stoneing about ten or twelve inches thick for a foundation); upon this wood is laid cast iron an inch and a half thick, a part of which weighs in every single yard forward 141 pounds, and other models weigh only 81 pounds; when the wagons come upon these roads, which together with the the limestone weighs in the sundry kinds of these carriages, they do, and have made use of, not less than four, five, and six tons, and I believe as much as seven tons even, which burden being laid upon all four feet in length, the above roads, although enormous in their first expence, are nothing too strong.

The early line was re-aligned a few years later, on a better, higher level, but was never very efficient. The re-alignment was made necessary because, by an Act of Parliament of 1783, the Caldon Canal was extended a further 530 yards from its original terminus to the west of the Ipstones road, near the Navigation Inn, now demolished. It was necessary to construct a tunnel under that road, and a further bridge under the Foxt road, to the present canal basin.

Let me tell you a story about this tunnel, Nithsdale, which you may have heard and which may or may not be true, but, like all good stories, is worth the telling. A certain canal boatman was instructed to take an empty boat from Etruria down to Froghall, and bring a full load back. But the old 'boatie' was warned that an empty boat would be too high in the water to pass under the Froghall tunnel. It was suggested that he take a boatload of his friends down to Froghall as human ballast, giving them a trip out at the same time. This he did, and when he was fully loaded and ready to return, he looked for his mates, and could not find them. It appears that every one of them had spent a convivial hour in the Navigation Inn and were in no fit state to undertake the journey home. How they eventually found their way back to the Potteries is not recorded!

Now, my friend WH, let us walk up the incline from the canal basin, passing the older limekilns, almost merged into the hillside, and observe the hefty stone footings of the old tramway winding drum at the head of this short incline. These huge drums provided the braking power for the loaded trucks going down, and the power for hauling the empty trucks back. Turning off the track to the right, by the old stone building, we find ourselves standing at the foot of the Great Froghall Inclined Plane, stretching steeply ahead of us, straight as a die, through the trees. This is part of the next tramway system, constructed in 1802 by the famous engineer, John Rennie, whose work in the Moorlands area also includes the construction of Rudyard Lake. This tramway followed a radically different line out of the valley, climbing steeply up this inclined plane, rising 250 feet in a distance of about 300 yards, towards the village of Whiston, where there was a smelting works. There were other inclined planes at Whiston and Upper Cotton before the line reached the quarries, all operating on the principal of trucks linked on an endless chain, with the full trucks descending pulling the empty ones back up the incline. Horses operated the level sections. The winding drum at the foot of the incline was housed in the building behind us. Ever striving for greater efficiency, some 47 years later another, more direct line was constructed. By this time railway building techniques were more advanced, and the engineers, by driving through cuttings and raising embankments, were able to build a line that both looked and operated more like a real railway than any of its predecessors. This 1849 line operated until 1920, by which time the limestone was being transported from the quarries by other means. As you so rightly commented:....

> *and yet in a few years, when the railway company gets working on the lower side of the great limestone hill above Waterhouses, it is certain to fall into desuetude; and the canal will either be drained, as a portion which formerly ran further down the valley to Oakamoor has already been done, or left entirely to fishermen, boy-bathers and suicides.*

THE CHURNET VALLEY has been referred to, with good reason, as the 'Hidden Valley' or the 'Secret Valley'. Perhaps it lacks the photogenic charm of the limestone dales nearby, but then it is not so 'open', so accessible to the masses. It is a very special place, it has an enchantment of its own, in its rich natural history and its complex industrial history, woven together by the threads of river and canal. To fully appreciate the valley, to gain an affinity with it, you need to visit its green and pastoral heart. Only then will its hidden secrets be revealed -the spirit of the place, as it were. But access is not easy, for whilst there are roads across the valley, there is no road through the valley; it has not become the domain of the motor car.

> *....... it is remarkable that no highway is to be found in this valley between Upperhulme and Oakamoor. The roads are all situated on the high lands above .... they have been probably constructed along the old mule tracks; and wherever one approaches or leaves a Churnet village, or crosses the valley, one is faced with tremendous banks, which inspire respect in the bosom of the most flippant traveller.*

As we leave Froghall we climb one of these 'tremendous banks', for we are heading for Kingsley, a large, sprawling village, carved into two halves by the busy main road which runs through it.

St.Werburgh's Church at Kingsley, with its solid tower, part of which is 13th century, is largely the work of Thomas Trubshaw, the Staffordshire builder and architect of the early Victorian years, who did much fine work. Built on the site of a much earlier church (1221) it was further altered in 1886, when a new porch was added and the chancel and vestry rebuilt. A fine impression of Kingsley church and its tower is found in this extract of a poem, written in 1920 by

Abraham K.Mosley, one of the unsung poets of the Staffordshire Moorlands:

> For o'er five hundred years and more,
>> Has Kingsley's tower crowned Kingsley Banks,
> Embattled, moss-grown, grim and gray,
>> A landmark score o'mile away;
> Guiding errant wanderers to their homes
>> And worshippers to Church.
> For centuries bronze bells have pealed
>> On Yuletide morn and New Year's Eve,
> Ringing in joyous mirth the call -
>> Peace and Goodwill and Joy to all.
>
> The Parish Church o' Kingsley's Tower,
>> A beacon fired with mother's love e'er watches o'er
> Whiston, Holt Cross and th' Moors
>> To Morridge snows and Cauldon's Lowe,
> O'er Churnet's Vale from Consall Wood
>> To Oakamoor and Alton;
> Ne'er idling lazily, but creaking,
>> Racking, straining beam and stone
> Its bells waft hallowed peals abroad;
>> And betimes speak a parting knell,
> 'Mid sighs and tears for loved ones gone before.

Kingsley has a number of buildings which are no longer used for their original purpose, but stand as memorials to former days of piety and godliness. These include both a Wesleyan and a Primitive Methodist chapel, and a Temperance Hall. In common with many moorland villages, the Primitive Methodist movement gained much support in Kingsley as it swept through North Staffordshire following its foundation by Hugh Bourne and William Clowes in 1807 at Mow Cop, another windswept hillside not so far away, where the first Camp Meeting was held on May 31st. As the Centenary Commemorative Plate, by Wood and Sons of Burslem, states:

> The little cloud increaseth still,
> Which first arose upon Mow Hill.

The villagers of bygone Kingsley, then, had their spiritual and cultural needs well catered for. Their social needs were equally answered by the local pubs, where the thirst created in mine or quarry was prodigiously satisfied.

WE MUST NOW BEGIN OUR RETURN JOURNEY to Leek, dear Nithsdale, so we follow what is now the A52 road, with its snorting quarry lorries, always anxious to make up lost time, and join the Cheadle road at Kingsley Moor, where the already heavy traffic flow is seasonally swollen by cars and coach-loads of visitors seeking the delights of Alton Towers.

I guess 'theme park' is a term new to you, WH. It is one of those peculiar phenomena of the late twentieth century which, alongside time-sharing, package tours, business parks, hypermarkets, shopping malls and shuttle services, has been created to show a profit for someone. In your day, my friend, life was much more simple!

But we must let the twentieth century take us to the crossroads at Cellarhead, where there was once a pub on each corner - four hostelries facing each other diagonally across the road, each seeking the passing traveller's trade. From here we go to Wetley Rocks, which has a spectacular outcrop of gritstone, giving the village its name, and reminding us that there was once quarrying in the area. The rocks are virtually the last southerly bastion of the rugged Pennines. The Mason's Arms was an old-fashioned pub which once stood in the shadow of the rocks, on the site of the present petrol filling station, so that where once the thirst of the quarry workers was quenched by good old English beer, now the demands of the internal combustion engine are similarly slaked. The Powys Arms opposite, and still trading, was formerly called the Arblasters Arms, thus commemorating the names of two former Lords of the Manor of Cheddleton. The Lord of the Manor was a powerful figure in rural society, for he was virtually the landlord of a large estate, retaining part of the land, called the demesne, for his own use, while the rest was either tenanted or regarded as common land or waste. His manorial holding commanded much respect in the parish.

WHEN WE REACH CHEDDLETON we realise that this is a village which has expanded greatly since the Second World War, having almost reached the status of a small town. New housing estates have sprung up on either side of the main road, and the growing population includes many commuters who travel to work in the nearby towns or the Potteries. How different from your first impression of Cheddleton, my friend:

From the summit of a bank over Cheddleton we were treated to a glorious summer evening panorama, with Leek some four miles in the distance, and the Roches forming a beautiful background still further beyond, while the sky effect was beyond my description. We jogged leisurely downhill into Cheddleton, left our car in charge of a small boy, and climbed up a steep bank to the church, which is well worth a visit; and inspected the remains of the stocks fixed in the wall opposite a 'Black Lion' of the public house order. We descended by a footpath to the canal bridge, and found a pretty view across a series of locks to the paper mill.

You reminded us there of two important features of Cheddleton's history - the church and the paper mill. The church is dedicated to Saint Edward, one of the comparatively few parish churches in England to be consecrated to the Confessor, although it is interesting to note that there is another but four short miles away in Leek!

'Well worth a visit', you said, my friend, so let us follow in the footsteps of a silent host of old villagers, up the hill to the church. Immediately we notice something different about the church doors - here, carved in the wood of the outer surface, are the figures of Saint Edward and Saint Edmund keeping a silent watch over the churchyard, where lie generations of old Cheddletonians, rich and poor, famous and workaday. Here lies Lady Elizabeth Wardle, wife of Sir Thomas Wardle and founder of the Leek Embroidery Society, and members of the powerful Sneyd family, alongside the paper workers, farmers and artisans, kept apart by society in life, but levelled in death. A moving reminder that war is also a great leveller is seen in a headstone near the porch wall. This incorporates the battlefield cross brought from the grave in France of Thomas Humphrey Sneyd, of Ashcombe Park, who was killed in action in the First World War at Ploegsteert on November 2nd 1914 - a mere nine

days before the Armistice. The cross was made by the men of his regiment, the 4th Battalion Lancashire Fusiliers.

Parts of the church date from the thirteenth century, but it is perhaps most notable for its stained glass, and it would be difficult to find better examples of the work of Morris and Co than these at Cheddleton. The Pre-Raphaelite influence is very strong, with the craftsmanship of Edward Burne-Jones, Dante Gabriel Rossetti, Ford Madox Brown and William Morris himself represented in the various memorial windows.

A rather more modern feature is the altar rail, installed in memory of a former vicar, the Rev.J.H.Bowman, who died in 1972. This is the work of the Yorkshire firm of wood-carvers, Thompsons, whose trademark is a little carved mouse - but you have to look very hard to find it!

Returning to the main road we emerge just below the row of old cottages which once rejoiced in the name of 'Babylon'. Why the name of this ancient city, synonymous with sin and depravity, should be applied to this part of the village is not known. Some would say that it was because of the iniquity and immorality which existed there, others that it was on account of the large numbers of babies born there, so it is perhaps a blend of the two - the latter being a consequence of the former!

Cheddleton, which today is making great efforts to attract the growing tourist trade, and may well be described as the 'Gateway to the Churnet Valley', was once very industrialised. Brittains Paper Works, famed for its production of India Paper on which thousands of Bibles and classics of English literature were printed, was known throughout the world. There was also weaving, tanning and brewing. The impressive water mill has been lovingly restored and is open to visitors, as is also the railway station. The Churnet Valley Line passed through Cheddleton, and, like most of the stations on the line, its buildings are a fine example of Victorian railway architecture. The work was attributed to the famous architect, Augustus Welby Northmore Pugin, by the late Poet-laureate, Sir John Betjeman, who played a significant part is saving the the station from demolition. It is now a well-run railway museum, and steam is back on the line!

A water-mill existed in Cheddleton as early as 1253. By 1580 there were two mills - a fulling mill and a corn mill. In the 1720s the miller was Ralph Wood, of the Wood family of pottery manufacturers in Burslem. There were two water wheels, the North Mill being built about 1770 to grind flint for the pottery industry. It is characteristic of the work of James Brindley, who besides being the surveyor of the Caldon Canal in 1772, also built a corn mill on the River Churnet at Leek.

There are two splendid cricket grounds in the Cheddleton area. The tree-girt ground belonging to St Edward's Mental Hospital must surely be one of the loveliest settings in the whole country for that most English of summer games. The nearby ground alongside the main road at Ashcombe Park has a more open aspect, with views over the surrounding countryside and a back-drop of hills. Keenly contested local league matches take place there during the season.

When I was a boy a trip to a cricket match at either of these two grounds was a great treat - not too far as to be inaccessible, but just within walking distance from Leek, if we couldn't afford the bus fare. And what contests there were in those days. Those matches of yesteryear seemed to capture the true spirit of the game, when the sun always shone and rain never stopped play. The close proximity of the teams meant that these 'local derbys' were keenly contested affairs, watched by large crowds. It was not unusual to see a constant stream of spectators walking along the Cheddleton road, by Birchall and Leekbrook, on their way to the match. And this is the route of course which we followed, my friend, at the start of our little outing, and the route which must now take us back to Leek.........

We trotted smartly by the dye-works at Leekbrook and quickly arrived at the gigantic railway bridge where, by the navvy settlement, we had turned unto the Basford Lane earlier in the afternoon. Another mile and a half up, past Sheep House, and down beyond Birchall, and up again to Cornhill Cross, brought us on to Compton and into Leek.

St. Edward's Church, Cheddleton, main door with the wooden figures of
St. Edward and St. Edmund

The Battlefield Cross of Major TH Sneyd, Cheddleton Churchyard

The moody, mysterious Mermaid Pool, Morridge

CHAPTER III

A DAY A-WHEEL

Thorncliffe, Blakemere, Newtown, Longnor, Sheen,Hartington,
Beresford Dale, Hulme End and Warslow

WE TAKE TO THE HILLS AGAIN, WH, for our next outing. The rugged, wilder parts of the Moorlands await us, as we leave Leek by the *'laborious'* Buxton Road, as you saw fit to call it. We will follow your preference for bicycles on this trip, but I think we shall find our mountain bikes more appropriate for the terrain than your old push bikes!

We soon leave the main road, as Leek slips behind us, and we turn right at the Moss Rose, to freewheel down to Cartledge Hollow. The luxury of a downhill road is soon surpassed, however, as we begin to climb towards Thorncliffe. This tiny Moorland community, where you observed a good deal of agricultural and commercial activity, has changed greatly since Edwardian times. The last survivors of this bygone age seem to be the pub, the chapel and the farms. The wheelwright's shop and the smithy have gone; we must rely on your keen observation, my friend, to remind us of how things were.

Thorncliffe we found to consist of a composite farm and public-house on the left; three farms standing cheek by jowl at a bend in the road a little beyond, with a letter-box as a sort of common property between them; then, at the foot of a small bank on the right, a little chapel; deep down on the left, a wooded ravine; a wheelwright's shop above; a cottage, and a smithy a few yards further along; another farm up another bank on the right; and yet another at the opposite corner of the cross-roads; while the round of the smithy corner revealed a hill-side that would put shame to many a house top.

Steep indeed is the climb up Thorncliffe Bank to the high ridge of Morridge, with ample excuses to stop for breath and admire the

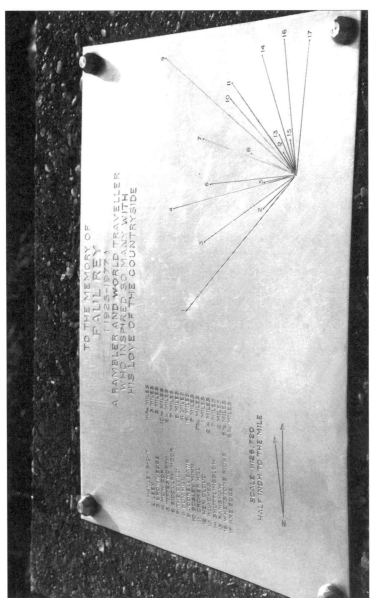

The Paul Rey Memorial on Morridge

panorama. This road affords many vantage points from which extensive views over the three counties of Staffordshire, Derbyshire and Cheshire can be obtained. We can stand by the memorial stone in the lay-by. The stone has been erected in memory of Paul Rey (1925-1977), described as 'rambler and world traveller, who inspired many with his love of the countryside'.

Standing at this high, windy spot, we can pick out, with the aid of the descriptive panel, the various features over a wide area of countryside. The craggy profile of the Roches in the middle distance leads the eye to the level Cheshire Plain stretching to the far horizon and the hills of North Wales. Modern technology now imposes itself upon the scene where, given the right conditions, the immense dish of the radio telescope of Jodrell Bank can be seen, an example of the great leap forward that science has taken since your time, my friend.

We now found ourselves among the purple heather-clad moorlands, looking across the deep valley of the higher Churnet to the Roches and Ramshaw Rocks; and high upon the opposite bank we saw the road by which we travelled to Buxton on Saturday. The prospect was exquisite, delightful; and we free-wheeled down the road to the "Mermaid" with our attention divided between the glorious panorama on our left and the intricacies of the rough road before us.........

The walk around Morridge was the great challenge to us as boys. You started, at a tender age, with the walk 'round the Mount', usually with your parents. You then progressed to a walk 'round Hillswood', then would come the hike 'round Gun' before graduating to the grand challenge of the Morridge ramble - an undertaking which would occupy us for a whole day. As most of the route followed lanes and roads from Leek we could hardly get lost, but what great times we had! We were warned to have nothing to do with the gypsies in Gypsy Hollow, but they never seemed to be there, so we passed safely through Thorncliffe and onwards and upwards to the exhilarating heights of Morridge itself.

The ridgeway across Morridge is a very ancient highway, likely to be prehistoric, and certainly very important in the packhorse days, carrying the ore from the old copper mines at Mixon down to the smelting works in the Churnet Valley. Travellers on this old road in bygone days would face dangers not only from the elements, where storm and tempest, snow and fog are a constant hazard, but also from man, for its very isolation provided a cover for dark deeds. Welcome indeed would be the old wayside inn, now known as the Mermaid, observed by you, WH, when you first came this way.

The "Mermaid" is a gaunt rectangular highland hostel and homestead of an extensive sheep-farm. It almost rivals the "Cat and Fiddle" in altitude, and, in other respects, in its isolation, its exposed position amid treeless moorland, and the severity of the winter storms, is quite as worthy of note........

Beyond the Mermaid Inn lies Blakemere Pool, sometimes known simply as the Mermaid Pool - one of those mysterious hill-top pools which appear to defy logic. Dr Robert Plot, writing in 1686, says this:

...the water is of the black-Meer of Morridge, which I take to be nothing more than fuch as thofe in the peat-pits; though it be confidently reported that no Cattle will drink of it, no bird light on it, or fly over it; all which are as falfe as that it is bottomleffe; it being found upon meafure fcarce four yards in the deepeft place, my Horfe alfo drinking when I was there as freely of it as I ever faw Him at any other place, and the fowle fo far from declining to fly over it, that I fpake with feveral that had feen Geefe upon it; fo that I take this to be as good as the reft, notwithftanding the vulgar difrepute it lies under.

Plot's 'vulgar disrepute' suggests that he was aware that this is a place of legends, of dark and scurrilous deeds. Plot makes no mention of the legendary mermaid of the pool, but, as we happen to be following in his footprints on this part of our journey, let us remind ourselves of your own observations, WH......

The pool is fabled as fathomless and the residence of a "Mermaid" who has furnished the neighbouring public-house with subject for its sign, and given colour to much superstitious folk lore in the immediate locality. The lady of this particular lake, when last interviewed by a mere man, asserted that when next she came from her mighty deep the waters would overflow and deluge the extensive vale of Leekfrith, right to the town of Leek, full four miles away. It is a pretty story, coupled as it is

*with statements that neither bird nor beast will drink of its
supposed brackish waters, particularly in these degenerate days
when astronomy has knocked the bottom out of heaven, and the
search for mineral wealth burrowed deep into the bowels of
hell; that a couple of dare-devil youths from Leek should
venture on its frozen surface one winter and dissipate its
sweetness by planting a very short stake into the bottomless
bottom. History hath it that the stake was left standing upright,
to the terror of the more credulous among the superstitious folk
in the country-side.*

You clearly had an ear for a good story, Nithsdale, but let me
tell you one which you missed. It concerns a local youth, a farmer in
these parts, whose parents were strict disciplinarians with high moral
values. The poor lad discovered that the young lady he was courting
had become pregnant. In the light of the bigoted standards of those
times he felt that he could not face up to his responsibility. Desperate
problems call for desperate solutions, so he decided that the best way
to ease himself out of his sorry plight was to get rid of the poor girl
once and for all, finally and irrevocably. He tempted her with the
promise of a night under the stars - an experience which they had
clearly enjoyed on at least one previous occasion - around the area of
Blakemere Pool, which would become her watery grave. The night
chosen turned out to be wild and stormy - a perfect cover for dark
deeds.

Meanwhile, that same night, at one of the inns in Leek, a group
of men were enjoying a convivial evening by a roaring log fire. The
conversation turned to the weather, and one man said: "It would take
a brave man to venture out onto the moors up on Morridge on a night
like this." Another man in the group then threw down a challenge,
saying that he would give £5 to anyone brave enough to walk the
moors of Morridge that night. The wager was taken up by one of his
friends, who set out on foot, promising to bring back some evidence
that he had completed the task.

As he approached Blakemere Pool he heard, above the howling
of the gale, the distressful cries of the poor girl, and realised that a
dark deed was about to be committed. In order to create a stratagem

Stormy skies over the Home Guard Memorial, Morridge

of deception and give the impression that he was one of several coming to the rescue, he called out, "Come on, Bob! Here, Bert! Now then, John, let's get him". The unfortunate youth, thinking that his number was up, dropped the girl and fled for his life. At this our brave and intrepid traveller rescued the girl, covered her torn dress as best he could, and took her back to the inn in Leek, presenting her as his proof that he had completed his task! So, my friend, if you should happen to walk into a pub in Leek with a pregnant girl in a torn dress, just try telling them that story!

When we were boys, striding these moorland trackways on our first real hikes, we were always aware of the dire warnings about the mermaid who lived in the pool, and who would beckon unwary wayfarers into her watery lair. These beliefs arose from another legend of the area, which told of a fair young girl who had been drowned in the pool as a witch. In due course, the local witch-finder who had condemned her was himself found drowned in the pool, with mysterious scratches on his face! We therefore always approached the pool with trepidation, but never did we see a shapely female arm rising from the murky depths. Our youthful imaginations, stimulated by Arthurian legends, were never fulfilled - we must seek elsewhere for our Excalibur!

THIS IS THE LAND OF SHEEP AND HEATHER, of curlew and grouse, of cotton-grass, heather and bilberry. And here, on the high point of these wind-swept moors, stands the Home Guard memorial. This small obelisk bears the names of former members of the 5th Leek Batallion Home Guard who died in the wider conflict of World War Two. The names are: Pte. Michael R.Stafford, Loyal Regt, L/BDrLeslie H.Horobin. RA, Gnr.Basil Cope, RA, and Marine Norman Y.Tatton, RM Commando. It would appear that the local 'Dad's Army' groups produced a breed of heroes! My father was in the Home Guard during World War Two. I seem to recall that whatever activities were indulged in on Sunday mornings meant that a good deal of sleep was necessary on Sunday afternoons. Military activities are still carried out in this area of open moorland, now frequently used for combat training exercises by army cadet forces and territorials. These week-end soldiers are based at the Blackshaw

Moor camp, formerly the home of the Americans, down on the Leek to Buxton road.

This is splendid cycling country. These were the roads, snaking un-fenced and un-hedged over the open moorland, which you followed with your companions, my friend, via Newtown and Fawfieldhead, to Longnor. As you rightly observed, neither of these two places can truly be described as villages, although there is evidence at Newtown that a larger community existed there in former days. There are the usual reminders - the stone-built cottages, the old Methodist chapel and the Anglican church, whose size indicates that they were built to serve the spiritual needs of a much larger population. Many of these moorland roads follow the course of old packhorse routes, and the severe winter conditions frequently experienced in this area call to mind the hazardous nature of the jagger man's way of life, where fog and blizzards would be part of his daily experience for many months of the year.

From Newtown by devious and hilly roads, indeed it is the hills which give such charm to North Stafford panorama, we cycled by Fawfieldhead - even more indefinite than Newtown, and then, turning sharply to the left along a pretty lane where we scared dozens of gambolling rabbits, we struck the turnpike along which runs the usual road, through Middle Hills, between Longnor and Leek.

THE ORIGIN OF THE NAME OF LONGNOR is generally reckoned to derive from 'Langenoure', meaning 'long ridge', and certainly this is an apt description of its geographical location between the upper valleys of the Dove and Manifold rivers. But Charles Masefield's 'Little Guide to Staffordshire' (Methuen, 1910) points out that in the Domesday Book it was called 'Longenarle', which means 'the tall alder tree', and this sounds much more engaging. If Longnor lacks pastoral, delicate charm, it certainly does not lack character. It has a gritty, rugged appeal, its old buildings being chiselled out of the local stone, so that houses and landscape display a unique harmony. Its former important status as the centre of this isolated area of the Moorlands is evidenced by the splendid Market Hall (1873), which dominates the cobbled market place. Its facade still displays the old toll board, recording the market tolls to be paid by buyers and sellers to Sir Vauncy Harper Crewe, Lord of the Manor of Longnor. You could have a stall six feet in length for four pence, each additional foot costing a penny. A pen of sheep, pigs or other livestock would cost you four pence, and if you were selling from a cart or carriage you would also pay four pence. Tolls to be paid by buyers were four pence for every horse, two pence for a cow or bull two years old and one penny if they were under two years old. A sheep was a halfpenny, and a pig one penny. Thus were the coffers of the gentry enriched.

St.Bartholomew's Church in keeping with its surroundings, is gaunt, plain and undecorated, with a pinnacled Gothic tower. It has a fine Venetian east window, and a Norman font. Built of local stone, the church dates from 1780. The churchyard is full of interest, with many unusual epitaphs on the silent tombstones. Notable amongst them is that of a local man, William Billinge, who, according to the words carved on his headstone, was....

BORN IN A CORNFIELD AT FAWFIELDHEAD 1679. AT THE AGE OF 23 HE ENLISTED INTO H.M. SERVICE UNDER SIR GEORGE ROOKE AND WAS AT THE TAKING OF GIBRALTAR, 1704, SERVED UNDER MARLBOROUGH AT RAMILLIES AND WOUNDED BY A MUSKET SHOT IN THE THIGH. HE AFTERWARDS RETURNED TO HIS NATIVE COUNTRY AND WITH MANLY COURAGE DEFENDED HIS SOVEREIGN'S RIGHTS AT THE REBELLIONS IN 1715 AND 1745. HE DIED WITHIN THE SPACE OF 150 YARDS OF WHERE HE WAS BORN AND WAS INTERRED HERE ON 30 JANUARY 1791 AGED 112 YEARS.

BILLETED BY DEATH, I QUARTERED HERE REMAIN
WHEN THE TRUMPET SOUNDS I'LL RISE AND MARCH AGAIN

These old epitaphs are full of rural lore and social history, and often give an insight into the old village trades and crafts. Samuel Bagshaw, a joiner who lived at Hardingsbooth, has this memorial which tells much about the man and his trade:

BENEATH LIE, MOULDERING INTO DUST
A CARPENTER'S REMAINS -
A MAN LABORIOUS, HONEST, JUST,
HIS CHARACTER SUSTAINS.

IN SEVENTY-ONE REVOLVING YEARS
HE SOWED NO SEEDS OF STRIFE,
WITH AXE AND SAW, LINE, RULE, AND SQUARE
EMPLOYED HIS CAREFUL LIFE.
BUT DEATH, WHO VIEWED HIS PEACEFUL LOT
HIS TREE OF LIFE ASSAILED.
HIS GRAVE WAS MADE UPON THIS SPOT,
AND HIS LAST BRANCH HE NAILED.

Tradition has it that he drove the last nail into his coffin, leaving only the lid to be screwed on! Samuel Bagshaw had a brother, Isaac, the village blacksmith, who died in 1799, aged 78. His epitaph, whilst not being exclusive to Longnor for it is seen on blacksmiths' headstones elsewhere, is worth recording as a piece of bucolic verse, for it would surely find a place in any anthology of graveyard poetry:

MY SLEDGE AND HAMMER LIE DECLINED;
MY BELLOWS, TOO, HAVE LOST THEIR WIND;
MY FIRE'S EXTINCT, MY FORGE DECAYED;
MY VICE IS IN THE DUST ALL LAID;
MY COAL IS SPENT, MY IRON'S GONE;
MY NAILS ARE DROVE, MY WORK IS DONE.

Sometimes these silent tombstones conceal a story that was both dramatic and tragic. Such was the case with Jane Simms - a rural tragedy that might have sprung from the pages of Thomas Hardy or the Brontë sisters:

DEDICATED TO THE MEMORY OF JANE SIMMS WHO UNINTENTIONALLY EFFECTED AN IGNOMINIOUS EXIT OF HER INGLORIOUS CAREER ON THE 21ST DAY OF APRIL, 1830, AGED 22 YEARS -

I PLACE THIS HERE KIND FRIENDS TO LET YOU KNOW
A SUBTILE LOVER PROV'D MY OVERTHROW;
PERFIDIOUS SUITORS ALL I DID BEWARE,
FOR DOOMSDAY SHALL THEIR SECRET DEEDS DECLARE,
AND THOUGH I'M VANISHED FAR FROM HUMAN VIEW,
YET AT GOD'S BAR I SURELY SHALL MEET YOU;
WHERE FEMALE WRONGS SHALL AMPLY BE REDREST,
AND FRAUD AND GUILE FOR EVER BE SUPPREST

It is recorded that this tragic death was effected 'in consequence of poison'. Longnor in bygone days was not without its moments of drama.

Longevity seems to be a feature of life in Longnor, with many residents living to a ripe old age. Perhaps this is due to the absence of major roads and atmosphere-polluting industries in the area, or maybe it's just the bracing moorland air. A death notice published in the Westminster Magazine of 1780 has this intriguing piece about a local man:

LONGNOR, NEAR BUXTON, DERBYSHIRE, SAMUEL FIDLER, AGED 105. He walked from his own house to Buxton within three days of his death, which is upwards of five miles.

One wonders if this was a regular walk for Mr Fidler. The terrain between Longnor and Buxton does not make for easy walking, and the trip may have speeded the end of the poor old man.

A unique experiment aimed at promoting the health and prolonging the life of the villagers took place at Longnor in the 1970s. A television company wished to produce a programme on smoking habits in a village community and chose Longnor as its setting. The idea was that all the pubs and shops in Longnor should withdraw cigarettes from sale for one week, during which time smokers would be almost forcibly encouraged to give up the habit. The experiment created much national interest, and Longnor enjoyed a period of media publicity. A significant number of people managed to give up smoking completely, and were the subject of a follow-up programme. It is not recorded whether the sales of beer and spirits in the pubs increased as the sales of cigarettes diminished!

Longnor was formerly a market town, proudly bearing the title of 'the Township of Longnor'. Your impression of this is very fitting, Nithsdale:

Verily here can be laid the foundation of the story of a man who, in a small market town one market day, queried, "Where is the market?" "Oh," he was told, "It hasn't begun yet." He then went into a pub for a drink. I do not know why it should be necessary to explain that when a man goes into a pub it is for a drink. Anyhow, this man had a drink, and when he came out he

again asked, "Where is the market?" "Oh," came the reply to
his amazement, "It's over."

AFTER THAT LITTLE 'NITHSDALE-ISM', my friend, we must
proceed to the nearby small village of Hollinsclough, nestling in the
valley, sheltered by Hollins, Chrome and Parkhouse. This is not a
firm of solicitors, but the names of the three hills to the north, which
afford some protection from the cold northern gales. You described
Hollinsclough, my friend, as an exquisite, out-of-the-world,
unconventional little village, possessing nothing of note, neither
parson, policeman nor pub, nothing historical but the famous river.
However, when we explore it a little deeper we can discover some
interesting facts about its history which you apparently failed to
notice. Hollinsclough has one of the oldest Methodist chapels in the
Moorlands. This sturdy stone building with ashlar dressings has
withstood the rigours of the local climate for nearly 200 years.
Above the door is a tablet inscribed: BETHEL:J.L.:1801. The well
proportioned interior has a large gallery at the rear, where in bygone
days musicians would play lustily.

The significance of the 'J.L.' on the outside tablet becomes
clear when we see the monument to John Lomas, 1823, and Sarah,
his widow, 1833. John Lomas was a remarkable man, and his story is
worth recounting. John Lomas, truly a man of the Moorlands, was
born at Alstonefield in 1747. His father was a hawker and pedlar,
travelling by packhorse routes to transport silk from Macclesfield
and cotton from Lancashire to places as far away as Lincolnshire,
Cambridgeshire and Suffolk - an early pioneer in the road haulage
business. He took his son, the eight year old John, with him, and later
John set up in business on his own account when he was just
seventeen. He married when he was 21, and it was the influence of
his young wife which led him into Methodism. This was the time
when the early Methodists held their meetings in cottages, and the
young couple, much against John's will, went to hear a travelling
preacher at Flash. The persuasive oratory of these early preachers led
John to a decision, on December 28th 1783, to devote his life to the
Methodist cause. Their home at Hollinsclough became a centre of
Christian activity for over 40 years. Towards the end of his life, John

Lomas built the chapel at his own expense, and he and his wife are buried beneath its floor. Throughout his life he travelled far and wide in the course of his business, but his heart was always in his beloved Moorlands.

The rather odd looking Church of St Agnes (1840) has an unusual two-storied porch, and a house built onto the west end. The bell turret is also uncommon, but perhaps typical of the somewhat quirky nature of Moorland culture.

FOLLOWING YOUR OLD ROUTE AGAIN, Nithsdale, we take the road to the south-east over Sheen Moor. The road runs past Race House - a name which might seem a bit incongruous in this Moorland setting, until we realise that there was a race course here in this remote spot in bygone days. There were a number of these isolated horse racing venues in the Moorlands, supported no doubt by the local farmers and landowners. These sites were usually located far enough away from the arm of the law to allow illegal gambling to be carried out with impunity. To the left of the road, in the valley of the River Dove, lies Pilsbury and Pilsbury Castle Hills. The earthworks of Pilsbury Castle can still be seen. This ancient site was a motte and bailey castle, possibly Norman or later.

On the far side of the valley are the hills of Waggon Low and Carder Low. There are many of these 'lows' in the area. It usually signifies the presence of a burial mound, a reminder of the long dead civilisation which peopled these green hills and well-watered dales in prehistoric times. There have been many important archaeological discoveries in this area of the White Peak, notably by a local man named Thomas Bateman, of Middleton-by-Youlgreave, who pioneered the work in Victorian times.

Sheen is a dainty North Stafford village, with an old market cross in front of the school. The quaintly built houses have grown by the roadside as if with a desire that none should associate with another. Sheen affords few facilities for gossiping housewives, and neighbours desirous of quarrelling can in but few instances do so without the one or other proceeding some little distance from their own doorsteps. It has a pretty church, with a peculiarly shaped tower, which, on the

Derbyshire side, is a landmark for miles around. There are several quarries in the immediate neighbourhood, Sheen stone being famed for durability.

Sheen is a village of great antiquity. The village cross which you noted, dates from the 15th century. There is also an ancient burial ground known as the Royal Low - yet another of the many 'lows' in the area. The fine Victorian church was built in 1852, the original architect, C.W.Burleigh of Leeds, being replaced by another man, Butterfield, on the instruction of Alexander Beresford Hope, of Beresford Hall, a rich, devout Anglo/Catholic, patron of the living. The church reflects the high church tastes of its patron, in its reredos, pulpit, altar and font. The large Victorian parsonage is also by Butterfield.

A remarkable story of true friendship has its roots in Sheen. Thomas Bassett of Sheen was a carpenter who, in the 1860s, emigrated to the United States, where he formed a close friendship with a Dorset man named Adolphus Frederick Bleathman. The two men pledged to honour their friendship to the very end, and respect each other's wishes. In 1867 Bassett was working on a house in Memphis, Tennessee, when he had a fall from the scaffolding. He broke his neck, and died as a result of the accident. Bleathman personally and at his own expense arranged for the transfer of the body back to Bassett's home village of Sheen for burial - no mean task in those days.

Sheen has leaped into prominence in recent times with the establishment of the engineering works, which, besides finding employment for many local people, has given a much-needed boost to the economy of this isolated area.

WE LEAVE SHEEN BY THE ROAD TO THE SOUTH of the village, turning left at the crossroads to join the road into Hartington near to Bank Top...........

Hartington is a pretty village surrounding a large open space like nothing so much as a barrack square, in one portion of which, all open to the road, is set an extensive duck pond.......and has a Hartington railway station a mile and a half

further in the wild uplands of Derbyshire. There are several
high-class boarding houses in the vicinity, and every summer
time brings Hartington its share of the holiday makers who
swear by the Dove.

And still today, my friend, if you wish to see the impact of
tourism on the Moorlands, visit Hartington on high days and
holidays. Now that the motor car has given people easy access to the
countryside Hartington has become a 'tourist trap' - with its
associated traffic problems, which a well-sited large new car park has
gone some way to ameliorate. Much of the attraction of Hartington
lies in its shops and teahouses, where traditional cream teas are
served. The tourist wishing to part with his money has ample
opportunities here - a walking stick for Grandad, a nice piece of local
pottery for Grandma, a sheepskin coat for Mum, a pipe for Dad, and
don't forget to sample the local cheese! Cream teas, gift shops,
hotels, pubs and holiday cottages all combine to give Hartington a
somewhat cosmopolitan air which belies its rural setting.

Not as rugged as some of its neighbouring villages, Hartington
has a more gentle charm. The picturesque village pool, complete
with waterfowl, is surrounded by broad grass verges. There is a well
which has its own traditional well dressing ceremony in the summer.
The village hall is in constant use for antique fairs and other shows.
Indeed, there is always something happening in this busy, bustling
rural centre. And even when the summer crowds have diminished
there will always be groups of hikers setting out to tramp the
surrounding hills and dales, whatever the weather.

The fine parish church at Hartington is dedicated to Saint Giles,
patron saint of cripples and beggars. It has some superb examples of
Early English and Decorated work, and a very ancient font which
will have witnessed the baptisms of countless generations of
Hartington babies. The tower, which dominates the village on its
elevated hillside, is 14th century, and the splendid reredos is
constructed of Derbyshire marble. The two lancet windows in the
north wall date from 1220, and there is a fine Perpendicular window
in the south wall. Other windows and features date from the Early
English and Transitional periods. The north transept is often referred

to as the Biggin Chapel because it was appropriated to the inhabitants of the nearby small village of Biggin, which is not on our route. There are old stories that, in bygone days, many horse-thieves lived in the Biggin area. Stolen horses, it is said, were hidden in underground stables until the hue and cry was over, when the animals were taken far away to be sold.

In Hartington churchyard is the family vault of the Sleigh family, where the Leek historian, John Sleigh was buried on 17 August 1907. Sleigh's great work on the history of Leek was originally published in octavo form in 1862 by the local printer, Robert Nall. A greatly improved and enlarged edition was published in 1883 by Bemrose and Son of Derby. This contained colour plates beautifully produced on heavy paper, and handsomely bound. There was a limited edition totalling 851 copies, sold to subscribers, comprising 602 copies bound in grey cloth boards, 234 copies on hand-made paper, bound in imitation leather, and a superb 15 copies only, leather bound. There cannot be many small towns of the size of Leek which can boast such a splendid local history. Allowing for its sometimes flawed research, Sleigh's History of Leek stands as a legacy from the time when Victorian men of means could indulge their enthusiasm in such a lavish way. *Requiesce in pace,* John Sleigh, your monument is your history.

Hartington was once served by the railway. Its station, however, on the Ashbourne to Buxton line, was about a mile and a half outside the village, to the east, entailing a steady, uphill walk to catch the train! This is one of the factors which sounded the death-knell for so many rural railway services - the communities the lines were intended to serve were often some distance from the nearest station! The line is now the Tissington Trail, a long-distance footpath open to walkers and cyclists. In the days of the railway, trackside embankments were always prime habitats for wild flowers, and now the railway has gone they remain so, making a walk along the track a bounty for botanists. And you are always likely to find the occasional fruit tree - apple, pear, plum or perhaps damson - which has blossomed from a core or stone thrown from the window of a passing train by a passenger who, having enjoyed his snack, would never know of the fruitful harvest of his action.

ACROSS THE LENGTH AND BREADTH of England there must be many towns and villages where you will find inns named after our great literary figures. The Upper Dove Valley can boast of two - the Charles Cotton and the Isaac Walton, thus perpetuating the memory of two immense, prodigious talents whom we shall meet as we visit Beresford Dale.

Returning towards Staffordshire, we left our bicycles at the mill below Bank Top and took the footpath into Beresford Dale....... *The walk along the beautiful river side with ever and anon a glimpse of a brown trout, was delightful. We saw the Charles Cotton Fishing House, said to have been built by Walton complimentary to Cotton, across the river just before we reached Pike Pool.*

Beresford Dale is one of the loveliest of the dales of the River Dove. Edward Bradbury, who passed this way before you, my friend, called it "Beresford's Enchanting Glen".

But we are at Beresford now, and passing over a rustic bridge are soon shrouded in the cool shade of luxuriant trees. Here is Pike Pool, with its curious pinnacle of rock from which it takes its name, and the rustic foot-bridge; here are pleasant grassy walks, towering tors, and lovely trees; and amid all the "Princess of Rivers" glides along, reflecting the pictures by which she is over-shadowed and surrounded as she passes on her peaceful way, broken occasionally by tiny waterfalls, the music of whose voices make a restful undertone to the song of birds.

What a perfect name for the Dove - the Princess of Rivers! You cannot think of the Avon without thinking of Shakespeare, the Lakes without Wordsworth, the Doon without Burns or the Tweed without Sir Walter Scott, nor can you think of the Dove without thinking of Charles Cotton and Isaac Walton - the two unlikely companions who found this 'marvellous pretty place' a rare delight. Isaac Walton's 'The Compleat Angler' is a classic of English literature, which succeeds on two counts - it reflects the Englishman's deep and abiding love of the countryside, its hills, its dales, its fields and its river valleys, whilst at the same time being a splendid treatise on the gentle art of angling, particularly for trout and grayling. It is full of good humour, good conversation and sheer love of life. It is a cheerful book, without a vulgar or jarring note, the epitome of a long-vanished England. The gentle, philosophical conversations between 'Piscator' and 'Viator' in the second part of the book take place beside the Dove, and the picturesque scenery of the district shines through the pages. You can never tire of 'The Compleat Angler'. With its sub-title 'the Contemplative Man's Recreation', it is a good book to take with you on the proverbial desert island.

You could hardly find two friends of more contrasting character than Walton and Cotton. It was the attraction of opposites, with Walton almost saintly and Cotton more profligate. Walton, born in 1593, was a Staffordshire man by birth, who married twice, his first wife being related to Archbishop Cranmer, and his second to Archbishop Ken. His sympathies during the Civil War lay with the Royalists, and he was a devout Anglican. For part of his life he was a draper in Fleet Street, London. He loved life in a gentle sort of way: "*I love such mirth as does not make friends ashamed to look upon one another next morning.*" Walton was the biographer of Donne, Hooker and Herbert, whist Cotton wrote the rather more earthy 'Virgile Travestie'. Walton's gentlemanly qualities were in sharp contrast with his good friend Charles Cotton, who was much more of a rogue by comparison. Born in 1630 at the nearby Beresford Hall, now demolished, he was described by Charles Lamb as 'the hearty, cheerful Mr.Cotton'. In Beresford Dale there is a cave called 'Charles Cotton's Cave', where, it is said, Cotton hid from his creditors. He is believed to have died in a garret in London at the age of 57.

The little fishing temple stands as a permanent memorial to the two friends. Here in this quiet vale, amidst this sylvan loveliness, Viator, in 'The Compleat Angler', was heard to say:

Stay, what's here over the door? PISCATORIBUS SACRUM. Why then, I perceive I have some title here; for I am one of them, though one of the worst; and here below it is the cypher too you spoke of, and 'tis prettily contrived...... I am most pleased with this little house of anything I ever saw: it stands in a kind of peninsula too, with a delicate clear river about it. I dare hardly go in, lest I should not like it so well within as without: but, by your leave, I'll try. Why, this is better and better, fine lights, fine wainscoted, and all exceedingly neat, with a marble table and all in the middle!

You would have suited their company well, Nithsdale. *"Let us take the good Nithsdale into our company, for he hath a sharp wit and a merry eye."* Sheer joie de vivre!

This is gentle walking country. On a stroll along the river bank to the appropriately named Pike Pool you are likely to see the dipper or the kingfisher. The curious and spectacular stone pillar is a natural feature - the geology of the area asserting itself amidst the natural history. And you are walking in the footsteps of Isaac Walton and Charles Cotton.

> *Pike Pool is beautiful! A deep pool of dark water out of which rises the perpendicular Pike Rock, all set in a wonderful sylvan solitude, and most enjoyable on a hot summer afternoon .... This North Stafford loveliness is most bewildering. It would be an almost impossible task for me to make any distinction even after but these three rambles, still at the time I thought Beresford Dale below Pike Pool the most charming picture my eyes have rested upon.*

With some reluctance we must tear ourselves away from the beauties of Beresford Dale, for the day is far advanced, and we must take the road to Hulme End. As the road approaches the riverside camping ground another road from Sheen joins from the right. Were you not intrigued, Nithsdale, by the small, square, walled enclosure in the field at the road junction? If you had looked over the wall you would have seen a small, wooded mound, with a yew tree, which might have suggested a burial place. The grave of some beloved pet animal, or even a small pets' cemetery? No, my friend, this was the last resting place of a local man, John Bonsall, who died over 200 years ago, and left a request to be buried on his own land. Clearly a man who loved the area so much that even death could not part him from his little patch of the Moorlands. Unlike the campers and weekenders who come in numbers to pitch their tents in the fields by the river, who are here one day and gone the next, Hulme End being just one more notch on their itinerary, another flag in their window. And so to Warslow.

YOU WOULD REMEMBER WARSLOW, my friend, as a typical
Moorland village, *'a sort of cross between Flash and Sheen'*. Now,
however, as you turn right for Leek, a row of houses has been built
on the left, obscuring the view of the church. These have the
appearance of belonging on an urban housing estate, which is a pity,
and the large modern school on the right does nothing to alleviate the
impression of town creeping into countryside. Nevertheless Warslow
still manages to cling on to many of its features of yesteryear - its old
pub, the Greyhound, providing welcome refreshment for all, its two
plain, unadorned old chapels, now put to other uses, its cluster of old
stone dwellings, homes of many of the erstwhile Ecton copper mine
workers and its fine Anglican church. The firebrand spread of the
Primitive Methodist movement into the Moorlands, and its
subsequent decline, is very apparent in the area, for barely two miles
away at Hulme End is another redundant Primitive chapel, and there
is one here in Warslow. The Wesleyan chapel at the top end of the
village survived longer, but it too has now become redundant.

The Church of St Lawrence is late Georgian (1820) with the
chancel by Charles Lynham being added in 1908. The interior is
interesting, with box pews, one of which would be reserved for the
squire and his family. There is a splendid stained glass window by
Morris and Co., in memory of Sir Thomas Wardle, who was a great
friend and supporter of Warslow church. Although this was installed
after William Morris had died, it serves to remind us of the great
association between the famous Victorian designer and Thomas
Wardle, the Leek dyer. In his later years, Wardle lived at the nearby
Swainsley, a large house in the Manifold Valley. It is apparent that
Morris would have visited Swainsley on a number of occasions, for,
in one of his last letters, written just before his death in 1896, Morris
writes, in a genuine moving tone, tempered by sadness, to decline an
invitation from Wardle to visit him:

My dear Wardle, It is very kind of you to invite me to share in your Paradise
and I am absolutely delighted to find another beautiful place which is still in
its untouched loveliness. I should certainly have accepted your invitation, but
I am quite unable to do so, for at present I cannot walk over the threshold,
being so weak. The Manifold is the same river, is it not, which you carried me
across on your back; which situation tickled us so much that owing to

inextinguishable laughter you very nearly dropped me in. What pleasant old times those were. With all good wishes and renewed thanks, I am, yours truly, William Morris.

Clearly Swainsley held very happy memories for William Morris. And here, in Warslow church, these Pre-Raphaelite images in the memorial window, are a reminder of that productive association between designer and dyer.

Let us now retrace your steps, WH, to the churchyard, where now we see the village war memorial. These simple stone obelisks and crosses have appeared in most Moorland villages since your time, but those were the golden years before Europe erupted in a blaze of fury, and the First World War claimed the lives of village lads from their homes and fields, their wives and sweethearts, and the old England which you knew, vanished forever.

A little bit of that old England still remains in Warslow, for Warslow Hall still stands, in its secluded position, just outside the village. It belonged to the Harpur Crewe family, from Calke Abbey, and we can imagine them taking their place in that box pew in the church on the Sundays when they were in residence at Warslow, for the hall would serve as a hunting lodge for their Moorland shooting forays. Great landowners in this Moorland area, they were typical of the 'squirearchy' which dominated rural England in those days.

With dusk approaching we must now return to Leek, following the open roads which brought us here this morning, passing once again the Mermaid, and descending steeply to Thorncliffe - a real test for our cycle brakes after the rigours of the day.

We stopped along the level at the top to admire the sunset, a superb spectacle of cloud and colour over-topping the grandeur of the Roches. It was a most impressive sight, and one worth an effort to see...... I enjoyed the remaining three miles, through Thorncliffe and the winding lanes in the waning light, as thoroughly as I did the whole day.

'Beacham's Pill' - Public Toilets, Mill Street, Leek

CHAPTER IV

MARKET DAY:
AND AN EVENING AT RUDYARD

LEEK HAS BEEN A MARKET TOWN for well over 700 years. Its original charter to hold a weekly market was granted in 1208, in the reign of King John. In many ways, Leek grew up around its ancient Market Place; it was the focal point of the town's development. The oldest buildings in the town can be found within a stone's throw of the Market Place. In many market towns the old parish church stands in close proximity to the market place, and this is so with Leek. The medieval pattern of streets around the church and Market Place is largely maintained today, and can still be traced in spite of the fact that road widenings, pedestrianisation schemes and one-way streets have been superimposed upon it.

The very names of some of the streets around the Market Place have a market connotation - Sheep-market, Dog Lane and Custard Street (now Stanley Street), probably so named as a corruption of the word 'coster', as this would be where you would find the costermongers selling their fruit and vegetables from barrows in a bygone age. Agricultural methods in the early days when Leek was gaining its market status would be primitive compared with the technology of today, but then, as now, there would be the requirement to buy and sell cattle and livestock, hence the need for a place where farmers could barter and bargain, haggle and harangue until they got the right price. This adroitness is part of the inherent character of any farmer, an inborn skill which has passed from generation to generation, and remains as much a symbol of his trade as the mud on his boots.

All this serves to remind us, my friend Nithsdale, that, after our toils around the countryside during the past few days, today we shall have a slightly less strenuous day, staying in Leek, for once again it is Wednesday - Market Day.

The normal condition of Leek is decidedly dull and sleepy.

Bargains and banter at Leek Market

Except at noon or at night, when the mill hands are abroad, its main thoroughfares are comparatively deserted. But this weekly Wednesday market brings a transformation. It is THE day of the week: a day of bustle and activity, brimful of incident, and one which makes regular life here tolerable. Leek is one of those old-world, old-fashioned markets, attended by old-world, old-fashioned people, which the march of modern civilisation, the railway train, the motor car, the electric tram and the prospective airship will some day relegate to things of the past. And Leek's market, because of Leek's peculiar and practically isolated situation in a highland country, will be one of the last to go.

Well, my friend, it hasn't gone yet, and although the pattern of Leek's traditional Market Day has altered greatly since the 1950s, before the cattle market moved to its new site off Junction Road, it is still the day when the country-folk don their Sunday best and come to town. The open-air stalls in the Market Place are an immense delight, and attract throngs of people. The old wooden stalls, with their canvas sheeting, have now been replaced by galvanised metal affairs with plastic covers, but the atmosphere remains, with the totters calling their wares, offering unbeatable bargains, verbally haranguing the shoppers - a cosmopolitan scene of hustle and bustle, from early morning until evening, trading in all weathers. Only in the most severe winter weather is the market called off. And who can match the prodigious, often raucous, sometimes ribald, sense of humour of the market folk?

There is always someone to talk to in Leek market, and you can have a deep and meaningful debate on the world and its problems, or just simply indulge in the latest gossip. Markets and fairs play an important role in the social history of any town - they are a traditional part of our way of life, a meeting place for buyers and sellers that has changed very little over the years - apart from the prices!

The Cattle Market always embodied the real spirit of Market Day in Leek. Before a purpose-built site was established on Smithfield, livestock were sold in the streets and on the open area in front of the old Talbot (formerly the Spread Eagle), which became

known as Sparrow Park and is now occupied by the Nicholson War
Memorial. The nearby Cattle Market Inn is aptly named, for it stood
on the very site. In 1874 a new site was laid out, bounded by
Ashbourne Road, Haywood Street and Leonard Street, and this
became Leek's Smithfield Cattle Market. It remained in use until
1960, when it was moved away from the centre of town to a new site
off Junction Road. The area then became the town's bus station, so
where once cattle wagons discharged their passengers you can catch
a bus to all parts of the Moorlands and beyond, or pick up your
holiday coach to sunny Spain. You, WH, arrived in the early
morning, in time for..........

> ....*the early arrivals - the butchers, cattle dealers, farmers and*
> *cattle - in the Cattle Market; and some funny specimens of men*
> *and animal we saw. Every man seemed to be armed with a stick,*
> *and when he had not both hands in his pockets with the stick at*
> *ease under his arm, he was belabouring some poor, inoffensive*
> *beast. Ever and anon we came across a man, now coaxing, now*
> *pulling, now shoving, and occasionally bodily carrying a*
> *refractory calf. We saw sheep driven in and brought by cart,*
> *pigs in traps and floats, and once in a while were alarmed by a*
> *rushing avalanche of potential beef, behind which were several*
> *shouting, gesticulating, stick-carrying creatures such as in*
> *calmer moments might pass for men. It was a veritable*
> *pandemonium.......*

What great characters these old cattle drovers were! Their
ribald humour, their vernacular language, their bucolic dress and
their undoubted cameraderie set them apart. They worked hard to
earn their beer, which they consumed in prodigious amounts. As a
workforce they were a rough and ready lot, but very adaptable and
very willing. A prince amongst this rare breed was one who rejoiced
in the name of Tommy Coldarse, or 'Cowdarse', in the local dialect.
As boys, we were always led to believe that we should regard him
under the more polite name of Thomas Winterbottom, but of course
we never did. Old Tommy was an extraordinary individual who had a
wonderfully colourful vocabulary. His command of an immense
variety of swear words had to be heard to be believed. We learned

more about the English language from old Tommy than ever we did in our English lessons at school. In those days there was an abattoir in Pump Street, just off Ball Haye Green, near our little primary school, and it was a common sight to see old Tommy driving a few cattle up the road from the market. He used a strong, knobbled stick to belabour the backsides of the poor beasts, particularly if one should wander off, and would no doubt have belaboured us with it if he could catch us, for he was the object of much taunting and baiting. Fortunately, with youth on our side, we were usually too smart for him, and managed to escape. Old Tommy and his earthy colleagues, hempen homespuns to a man, added much colour to the old Cattle Market ambience. They were as much a part of the smells and sounds of the market as the cattle themselves - indeed, the whole thing could not work without them. They were the well-oiled cogs in the complex machinations between dealers, farmers, butchers and auctioneers. And at the end of the day, when all the business had been completed, the men would put on their leather aprons and rubber boots and swill the faecal matter left by the animals down the drains, leaving the cobbled surface of the cattle pens clean and bright - until next time.

A lot of the 'character' of old Leek disappeared when the cattle market was moved to its new site off Junction Road in 1960, and with it went the old cattle drovers. Nowadays it is all very technical and clinical, with deals completed in comfortable offices, and cattle lorries waiting to transport the livestock to farm or abbatoir. Neither does the annual horse fair still exist. The working horse is a rare sight on the farm today, horses usually being kept as pets by the children of the farm, who might dream of one day becoming a champion show-jumper. However, your little story of the old horse fair is worth recounting, my friend, when you told of ....*a row of raw-boned things with straw-bedecked tails. "'Ow much?" asked a bucolic individual of a dealer beside such as row. "Which on 'em?" "Oh," indifferently; "Any on 'em." "Three pounds ten." "Bring that 'un out." "Nay lad, not 'im. Tha con 'ave any other but 'im." And then, confidentially: "Ah darna shift 'im. They're all reared agen 'im."*

Is not local dialect a wonderful characteristic of English life, adding some light and shade to our language? Your little story, with a number of examples of our native North Staffordshire tongue - 'any on 'em.', 'Tha con 'ave'..., 'Ah darna shift 'im...' - and so on, show how, far from demeaning our language, dialect actually enhances it, providing the nuts and bolts, as it were, of our culture, giving it a raw poetic quality. The dialect of your native Scotland is full of such rude eloquence; no doubt that is why you appreciated and assimilated so much of ours during your years in North Staffordshire. Our dialect is full of surprises. You don't play a violin with a 'bow' - you kick it around a football field. A 'wick' doesn't burn in a lamp or a candle - it lasts for seven days. 'Pee' means pay, so 'a wick's pee' might cause you to wonder, until you realise that it is your weekly wage! 'Cost' and 'shot' are not what they seem, but rather, 'can you' and 'shall you'. And what do you make of 'grind' and 'bonk'? Why, 'ground' and 'bank', you may be surprised to learn! The North Staffordshire dialect is better spoken than written, indeed, it often defies the written word. You have to say "If they canst kick this bow ite o th' grind Ah'll gi' thee a wick's pee", in order to understand it. And what do you make of this : "Ananyonyeranyonyer"? Our local language also has a number of unique words. 'Bullyragging' is a wonderfully descriptive word for a good telling-off or harrasssing, and a 'rapatag' is an idle, worthless person, who could well be the butt of a bit of bullyragging. 'Skrike' means to cry and sob, and 'jonnock' sets everything to rights, all fair and square. 'Moither' is another graphic word, for when we are 'moithered' we are in a bother, or, as we might say today, in a flat spin. And 'lozack' is to lie in an idle posture, 'lozacking around', spending the day in recumbent idleness. The phrase 'as idle as Litheram's dog' takes a bit of understanding, until we realise that, as the saying goes, this particular dog lay down to bark! But who the mysterious owner Litheram was, no-one seems to know.

It would be a sad day for England if all our rich regional dialects were to disappear, and our language become a standardised amalgam of so-called 'correct English', for dialect is the music of the regions, and the colourful conversation of our farmers on market day, and the locals in our factories, shops and pubs is an essential element in the character of the North Staffordshire Moorlands. Long may it remain so!

THE ANIMAL SMELLS of the old cattle market gave way, once a year, to another set of smells, when the annual May Fair pitched on the site. The acerbic smell of carbide on the Dodgems, the pungent smell of oil and grease from the Waltzer, the choking fumes of the Wall of Death mingled with the sickly sweet smell of candyfloss and the greasy smell of hot-dogs all evoke memories of the May Fairs of yesterday. Nowadays canned music, electronic amusements and modern motive power have taken away some of the old-fashioned fun. The Smithfield Cattle Market site in Leek was transformed for one long weekend each May into a fairground of merrymaking and revelry, with the arrival of Pat Collins' travelling fair.

Another old Leek tradition which seems to have died out was that of 'Chalky-back Day'. On the day the fair arrived in town, and whilst the various amusements were being erected, hoards of children would descend on the site and chase madly around, chalking on each other's backs. Your parents usually made sure you were wearing the oldest of old clothes, you equipped yourself with a good supply of chalk, usually stolen from school behind the teacher's back, and you were ready for 'Chalky-back Day'. And then the pursuit was on, the lads chasing the girls and vice versa, and when you were caught you were given a good rub down with chalk on your back, or worse, the rudest words your captor could think of were chalked there for all to see. The secret was to avoid capture, which you never did - hence the fun! Today youngsters can just buy a tee-shirt with the words already printed on in clear, bold type, so the game has become unnecessary, and the chalk can stay where it belongs, I suppose.

SPARROW PARK WAS THE SPLENDID NAME for this area of old Leek, where the cattle market site loosely spilled over to include the area now occupied by the Nicholson War Memorial, the 'Monument', as Leek people know it.

You described very vividly, my friend, the motley variety of street entertainments which you witnessed around Sparrow Park, but let me take you back a little further. In the late Victorian years this is where the 'Rag and Stick' travelling theatres pitched their wagons and performed for the people of Leek. They came to town with their large, flat-bodied wagons, which were set side by side, forming a platform, and the whole structure was enclosed by a large canvas covering to create an auditorium in which plays were performed. The repertoire of these companies of travelling thespians was varied, ranging from the most heart rending Victorian tragedies, which would have the audience booing and hissing at the dastardly deeds of the villain and sobbing for the poor unfortunate heroine, to the more uproarious farces, which would send the audience home deliriously happy. These plays were well supported by the folk of Victorian Leek, and I imagine that the more 'hammy' the acting the better the audience liked it. Today they wouldn't stand a chance in the face of the more polished and sophisticated performances pumped into our homes by the television, and they would be booed and hissed off the stage. Perhaps we have all been spoiled by too much 'canned' entertainment?

The 'Monument' is a great Leek landmark, WH, which was built after your time here. It is a splendidly proportioned First World War memorial, given to the town by Sir Arthur and Lady Nicholson in memory of their son, Lieutenant Basil Lee Nicholson and the many other local men who were killed in that great conflict which erupted in Europe so soon after your time in our area. It was a practice in the First World War for men to enlist together on a local basis, and the Old Leek Battery was no exception to this rule. This meant that pals from the same town who grew up together and went to school together, marched off to war side by side, and often died side by side. The many names engraved on the tablets around the base of the Monument bear testimony to the fact that few families remained untouched by the war. The names of the battles in which the men fought can be seen around the four sides of the obelisk, above the clock. In your day here, my friend, these were just names on a map, faraway places in France or Belgium which no-one had heard of. Now, together with Mons and Passchendael, they are etched into our history, as permanently as the letters cut into the Portland stone of Leek's Monument - HODGE, LOOS, YPRES, LENS, GOMMECOURT, SOMME, BELLENGLISE, RAMICOURT, BOHAIN.

The Monument clock, known by older Leek folk as 'Sir

Arthur's Wristwatch', has looked down on the heart of Leek since 1924. Beneath its benign gaze has passed many of the old 'characters' of Leek, who have taken their ease on its conveniently placed seats and watched the world go by. Men whose working lives were over, giving them unlimited time to kill, and men who should have been working, but who somehow managed to avoid it, gathered to talk the time away. "Who's dead or dying ...... who's run off with who ...... how's your back ...... what's the world coming to......it's about time the council sorted things out ...... when are we getting more pension ...... what a shocking match, and a lousy referee .... what a price tobacco is ...... the weather gets no better .... young folk today ...... and just look at her."

Come Saturday night, and these same men gathered at the little newspaper shop in an old cottage on Pickwood Road, awaiting the arrival of the 'Evening Sentinel, Football Final'. Here they would gather round the roaring fire, replaying the afternoon's match, steaming in their wet overcoats, smoking their pipes and spitting in the fire, creating such a fug that you might think you were in a sauna in Hades. Battered old prams and crudely constructed wooden barrows stood outside the shop, like a cluster of cars in the breaker's yard. But these rude chariots would come into their own next day, when they were trundled around the town by the lads delivering the Sunday papers.

Old prams were useful delivery vehicles in those days, my friend, providing transportation for a wide variety of goods, from bags of coal or coke to small articles of furniture and carpets. A familiar sight around Leek was old Chris pushing his battered black pram filled with all manner of mysterious bundles. Nobody seemed to know very much about old Chris, but everybody knew him, and he appeared to know everybody, for he had a cheery smile and a word of greeting for everyone he met. His lined and weathered face would break into a broad grin, and his eyes would twinkle as he cheerily saluted you, hailing you across the street if necessary. He seemed to survive by earning the odd shilling or two running errands for people, and was willing to take on anything within his capabilities, but no-one really knew what went into that old pram, and nobody asked any questions! And off he would go, pushing his pram down

'Sir Arthur's Wristwatch' - the Nicholson War Memorial, Leek

the streets of memory. A true individual, Chris was one of the old 'characters' of Leek.

Your memories of Leek, WH, were very vivid, filled with the teeming life of the town as you saw it. Much has been written about the architecture and history of Leek - the public buildings, churches, shops, factories and schools - but we are concerned with putting flesh, as it were, on the bones of history; not just the bricks and mortar, but the lives lived out within the fabric. So whilst we are in Leek, let us turn our attention to Derby Street. Today Derby Street has only a few local traders, unlike in your time, my friend. Company shops, pubs, offices, banks and building societies prevail. The local traders are in the minority now, but fortunately Leek has been spared too many 'corporate images', and much of the old spirit of the place remains. Leek folk loved the little shops; you knew where you were with them, somehow.

Let us, then, look back to a time when you could enter a shop and be fairly certain to meet the person whose name was on the board outside. Men like Edgar Deville in his butcher's shop, big and bluff and cheerful, his broad red face usually wreathed in smiles, with a friendly greeting for all, the knife or chopper brandished in his hand being merely the tools of his trade, rather than offensive weapons. Leek has always had a great reputation for pork pies of quality, and in any league table Deville's pies would stand very high.

Mr Skinner's shop-front was always festooned with pots and pans, besoms and brooms, shovels, rakes and spades, barrows, tools, bowls and sieves and all the paraphernalia of the ironmonger's trade. What a task it must have been for the assistants, always male, to put this lot out in the morning and bring it all in before closing time.

Fred Hill's bookshop had a very low ceiling, so that you could easily reach the top bookshelves. Outside, the large 'Onoto the Pen' sign told you that he was also a stationer, and from his vast stocks of pens and nibs and inks the individual's needs could usually be met. This was the shop where you bought your first fountain pen when you went up to senior school. This was where you bought your 'Biggles' books and the eagerly-awaited next issue of 'Boy's Own Paper'. The various boys' comics - 'Hotspur', 'Rover', 'Adventure', 'Wizard', and so on - were an endless delight, and the exploits of

Rockfist Rogan and the stupendous achievements of the mighty Wilson kept us on the edge of our seats. Fred Hill was a man of many parts, being also a newsagent and printer, as well as finding time for public work on the town council and other local organisations.

These old traders seemed to possess a boundless energy, and many were deeply involved in the running of the town. If you were fortunate enough to meet him in person you would find a small, rather Pickwickian character, with a twinkle in his eye, a ready wit and a cheerful smile. (How did these old shopkeepers manage to be so jolly all the time?) The printing works of Fred Hill was at the end of the cobbled courtyard opposite to the shop. Officially this was Court No.1, but it was generally known locally as Getliffe's Yard. Like many of these courts in Leek, it was once a row of workers' cottages. The houses were three storeys high, and the families lived in the upper rooms and kept domestic fowl on the ground floor. The printing works was established in three of the old cottages, which were converted to a workshop, in the early 1900s. Traditional letterpress printing was carried out by highly skilled journeymen craftsmen who took a great pride in their work. Here, in a workroom heated by an enormous coke-fired, pot-bellied stove which glowed red-hot at times, the work was done, under the fixed gaze of the lordly cast iron eagle which crowned the very impressive and ancient Columbian printing press on which posters were printed, advertising a range of events from election meetings, property sales and plays to cricket and football matches.

Morton's jewellery and watchmaker's shop stood on the site of Leek's old workhouse, with a courtyard of tiny, terraced workers' cottages behind it. Morton's Yard, as it was called, was a little community of houses just off Derby Street. These humble dwellings housed the families of silk workers, household servants and washer-women, and each house had its own little garden plot, which would no doubt supply the vegetable supplies for the families for many months.

Morton's shop was a delight. When you opened the door it was like stepping into a time capsule, for you entered a world of dark, plush, velvet-lined cabinets, the sanctuary-like silence being only broken by the gentle chorus of the many ticking clocks around the

walls. And into this inner sanctum would appear one of the two
Misses Morton - usually Miss Molly - who had a tremendous
knowledge of the trade, and who would tell you the current prices of
gold and silver at the drop of a hat. This little Victorian corner of
Leek retained its distinctive atmosphere for many years, but now the
site has been redeveloped, and the old shop remains as just a memory
to those who were privileged to know the Misses Morton. The two
sisters, Molly and Fanny, might have stepped out of the pages of a
Victorian history book, but in their own way they were very shrewd
and astute. Being strategically placed on the main street, and not
going to bed very early, they were in a unique position to observe any
untoward behaviour, and telephone the police, should trouble break
out, which happened rather frequently.

Bayley's ladies' outfitters shop was one of those mysterious
places which small boys never went into. They sold those mystifying
items known collectively as 'foundation garments', rejoicing in such
glorious names as LenaLastik underwear, Lenawooly vests and
knickers (light, warm and well shaped), Dracolena corsets, Fitu
slimming corselets ('the secret of figure beauty') and Brettle's fine
silk stockings - names which seemed to evoke the poetry of women's
underwear!

Tatton's bakery and confectionery shop and café was another
bit of Old England. The mock-Elizabethan style shop front, erected
in 1927, blended perfectly with the half-timbered Roebuck Inn next
door, making a street scene that was both pleasing to the eye and
aesthetically good. Here, in the calm of the café, withdrawn from the
busy street outside, genteel ladies in their Conservative hats would
sip their afternoon tea, chattering like birds and daintily feeding, not
on bird-seed, but on rich cream cakes and jam scones. Immaculate
waitresses in their starched white aprons and high-collared dresses
would attend to their needs, with only the tinkling of spoons in
teacups to disturb the chatter. At Tatton's you could buy the
Celebrated Leek Finger Gingerbread - the gingerest gingerbread that
ever there was - for two shillings a one pound tin. Made from a secret
recipe that no-one has ever discovered, this was a much sought-after
delicacy which had a great reputation far beyond Leek itself. A
hallmark of the shop was that Mr.Tatton was a firm believer in

quality, always insisting that everything he bought, made or sold should be of the highest standard of quality obtainable.

No-one walking from Derby Street to St Edward Street via Stanley Street could fail to be drawn to the old Penny Bazaar. This was probably Leek's first 'walk-round' shop, all the goods being on open display on the flat counter tops. With further items packed on the shelves around the walls, it was the place for bargains. As you passed around the shop there was a glorious mingling of smells - oil, paraffin, wax, polish and soft soap, that oleaginous, oily mass which would put a shine on many a tiled front door step. And overseeing the entire shop was the formidable Mrs Breaks, the proprietor, whose all-seeing eye was much more effective than modern closed circuit television. It was an exciting shop for small boys, but woe-betide you if you stepped out of line and incurred the wrath of Mrs Breaks. Here within reach were books, toys, crayons, paints, models, games, balls, bats, tops and whips, chemistry sets and stink bombs. You could hold lovingly in your hand that perfect model Spitfire. Then your reverie would be shattered by a piercing voice in your ear, "Those are three and twopence halfpenny, and you must put it down if you're not going to buy it!"

BEFORE WE LEAVE LEEK, Nithsdale, let us take a look at St Edward Street, a street no doubt well known to you, and perhaps little changed. Described in the Staffordshire volume of Nicholas Pevsner's 'Buildings of England' series as 'possibly the finest street in Leek', St Edward Street displays a wide variety of periods and styles of architecture. There is no common roof line - the intermix of gables, ridges, eaves and chimneys creates a harmony out of the disorderliness, and there is not a jarring note. The social history of St Edward Street is the social history of Leek. Here, in the big houses on the western side of the street, have lived a number of Leek's prominent citizens - silk manufacturers, professional men, lawyers and business men. Sleigh, Wardle, Challinor, Strangman, Allen, Worthington, Goodwin - these are all names associated with the big houses in St Edward Street. Many of these houses had extensive terraced gardens at the rear, where gentility would take its afternoon tea on the shaded lawns. At the other end of the social scale, in the tiny terraced cottages in the courts and alleyways leading off the street, lived the working-class families of those who earned their living in the silk mills owned by their near neighbours in the big houses - the entire spectrum of society, as it were, living within a stone's throw of each other. Jacob's Alley, Post Office Yard, the old Globe Yard and the little cobbled courts housed a microcosm of the citizens of Leek - honest working men, ragged-trousered children, cleaners, road sweepers, washerwomen, drunkards, wife beaters, rogues, wanton wenches and ladies of the night. A present-day sociologist would find old St Edward Street a rich area for his studies. There was no shortage of drinking places in St Edward Street. The long-vanished Cheshire Cheese, Black Lion, Wheatsheaf, Globe and Lightfoot's Vaults were well patronised in their day.

An amusing story about the Quiet Woman is recorded in that motley collection of disjointed pieces about old Leek which Matthew Miller gathered together and published in his 'Leek Fifty Years Ago' (1887). From this collection we pluck this little gem:

Some of our readers will remember the Quiet Woman Inn, when its swing sign represented a headless woman, with a necklet of blue beads, white muslin dress, stockings and saucy sandals. Two commercials, known then as 'outriders', were one night staying at the Red Lion, when John Barlow was the landlord. One bet the other a bottle of wine that he could show him "the quietest woman in Leek". Sallying forth arm in arm they went down Custard street and Spout street to the Quiet Woman, and one said to the other, pointing to the sign, "There is the quietest woman." "Yes", said his companion, taking him to the other side of the sign, "but there's another just as quiet". The proposer admitted that he had lost, and they returned to the Red Lion and consumed the bet.

It is unusual to find two pubs next door to each other, but we have it in St Edward Street, with the Quiet Woman and the Unicorn standing side by side. At the top of the street, beneath the unerring gaze of the Old Church, the Swan and the George used to face each other across the road, before a road widening scheme swept away the George. Along with the George went memories of the old coaching days, when coaching inns proliferated along this stretch of Church Street, up to and including the Market Place. The George was a hostelry of some renown, for it boasted 'the best stabling between Manchester and Derby'. In its latter days the George served as a meeting place for a variety of clubs and societies, and the music of traditional and modern jazz, folk songs and dances and ribald rugby songs reverberated around its ancient walls. And so, Nithsdale, with the broad prospect of Mill Street before us, directing us out of town, we will end our day in Leek as you did, my friend, and make our way out to Rudyard.

APPROACHING MILL STREET from Church Street we see a splendid little building to our left, on the road junction at the top of the hill. Octagonal in shape and built of red brick, its sightless, opaque round windows are set in stone. Its slightly curved grey roof sweeps gently upwards to a mini 'Italianate campanile', a puppy to its nearby big brothers on West Street School and the Big Mill further down Mill Street, as if its designer was trying to emulate the larger scale work of his Victorian forbears. This little gem is a public toilet, you may be surprised to learn, for it was not there in your day, Nithsdale. It is the work of W.E.Beacham, the council surveyor, whom we encountered when we considered the Haregate Housing Estate in our earlier chapter. For many years it was known affectionately by Leek folk as 'Beacham's Pill'. What a gem, a pearl amongst more prosaic public conveniences; a relief station *par excellence*.

When you reach the bottom of Mill Street, at its junction with Belle Vue and just opposite to the James Brindley water-mill, there once stood a little sweet shop. When I was a boy this was your last stop for sweets and ice cream before Rudyard. Here we would fortify ourselves with sweets and chocolate to sustain us on the next couple of miles or so on our walk to Rudyard. Coils of liquorice like bootlaces, and packets of sherbet powder were always great favourites - the former would make your nose and lips black and sticky, and the latter, really intended to be mixed with water, when consumed by the mouthful, would fizz and froth and foam gloriously in your mouth. The mixture of sherbet and liquorice was a truly lethal combination!

We continued our stroll on to the Macclesfield Road, and

beyond Bridge End took a footpath across the fields to the left,
and by fields and the feeder side walked to Rudyard.

As we follow the footpath into the fields we can look back across the Macclesfield road towards Highfield, and perhaps hear the impact of bat against ball and a round of gentle applause, for this is the local cricket ground, where that most princely of summer games has been played for over 150 years. (How many salmon and cucumber sandwiches must have been consumed over that period of time?) But the area could have been the venue for a much wider range of sporting activities if a certain group of Victorian entrepreneurs had had their way. Kelly's Post Office Directory of 1868 says:

> Highfield park was taken on lease for seven years by a party of gentlemen, who formed a committee, for the purpose of forming a recreation ground: it is situated about 1 mile from the town, and a charge of 1d is made for admittance to the grounds. A small grand stand has been erected here, it being the new race course for Leek races. Bowling, croquet, swings, archery, dancing, athletic sports and occasional fêtes render it the favourite resort of all parties.

Also, a contemporary issue of the 'Staffordshire Advertiser' newspaper reported as follows:

> The committee have worked with great zeal, being determined to ascertain if, under a spirited management, a 'Belle Vue' would pay in Leek.

As events turned out, this was an over-optimistic opinion, and Leek was saved from having a 'fun park' on its outskirts - the only sporting activity which has survived at Highfield being cricket. And we, my friend, can leave the busy main road by the stile just past Rock House, and enjoy our walk through the fields, passing under the old railway line, which in your day, would be busy with steam trains, to join the feeder path to Rudyard.

This has been a favourite walking route to Rudyard for generations. Honest shopkeepers and decent factory folk have walked these paths with their families, and now their children come with their own families along the time-honoured pathways. In the procession of walkers, after the families with their butterfly-chasing children had gone home, would come the courting couples, pausing perhaps in the warm twilight of a summer's evening, to enjoy an amorous dalliance in the long grass, which they would leave pressed flat - always, it seemed, in a perfect circle! The feeder itself, of course, is a man-made waterway. In 1796 the Trent and Mersey Canal Company decided to promote the idea of constructing a branch from the main line of the Caldon Canal near Endon to the town of Leek. Local manufacturers had been agitating for this for some time, and the scheme would entail the building of a reservoir at Rudyard for the purpose of providing a water supply for the new canal and for topping up the main line in times of drought. From the lake at Rudyard, the feeder follows the valley of the River Churnet in a great sweeping arc of three miles or so to the west of the town of Leek, to join the canal at Barnfields - a man-made water course in a natural valley. The valley sides to the west rise steeply, and are well wooded, with Cowhay Wood and Longsdon Wood a haven for wild life. Indeed, a section of the woodland has now been designated a wildlife reserve. The broad floodplain of the river is good farm land, and a golf course has been developed at the southern end. The more gentle slopes rise towards the town, where the new Westwood and Wallbridge housing estates mark Leek's western edge, with Westwood Hall, now a school, hidden by trees. The feeder flows gently along, bugs and water boatmen scavenging its surface, its banks lined with bluebells in the spring.

NOW WE COME TO RUDYARD, my friend. Rudyard has a unique ambience which is found in no other village in the Staffordshire Moorlands. There are virtually no ancient buildings within the village itself, no early church or old coaching inn. You won't find a village green, time-worn stocks, preaching cross or village pound. Rudyard is not that kind of place. Instead, you find a number of good, solid, soundly built Victorian residences, looking more like town houses and seeming somewhat incongruous in their inherently rural situation. Hotels that would not be out of place in an urban location, symbols of the affluence and gracious living of a bygone age, stand in the place of the traditional village pub. Sturdy stone villas, solid middle-class dwellings standing in their own wooded grounds and a sound, stone-built Methodist chapel with an impressive west window complete the scene.

Rudyard owes its status and prosperity to the presence of the lake and the coming of the railway. The North Staffordshire Railway Company were quick to exploit the picturesque setting of the lake, and having the means to transport people from afar, they were instrumental in establishing Rudyard as a popular Victorian and Edwardian playground, visited by many thousands on high days and holidays.

Amongst the visitors in the early summer of 1863 was John Lockwood Kipling. Born in Yorkshire in 1837, son of a Methodist minister, he was then working in Burslem as a pottery designer for Pinder, Bourne and Co. This artistic young man became a good friend of the Rev. Frederick Macdonald, a Methodist minister in Burslem, who introduced him to a group of like-minded, artistic young people. John Kipling was invited by his employer's daughters, the Misses Pinder, to join them on a picnic party to Rudyard Lake on this fine summer's day in 1863. Also in the party were the Rev. Frederick Macdonald and his sister Alice. The magic of Rudyard must have weaved its spell, for two years later John Lockwood Kipling married Alice Macdonald in London on 18th March 1865. Immediately after the wedding ceremony, the newly-married Kiplings sailed for India, where John was to take up an appointment as head of a new art school in Bombay. Their first child was born in Bombay on 30th December 1865. The boy was named Joseph, his grandfather's name, and Rudyard, to commemorate the affection his parents had for the place where they first met. Rudyard Kipling became one of the foremost writers and poets of the later Victorian years, eventually to be honoured with the highest award a writer can aspire to - the Nobel Prize for Literature. Thus did the name of Rudyard become known throughout the world.

RUDYARD WAS ALWAYS OUR 'BIG DAY OUT' when we were young. In those days, when travel was not so easy as it is now, it was your great treat, to spend one of those seemingly never ending idyllic summer days by the lake. The highlight of the day was a sail on the lake. There were many different vessels offering to take passengers, and if you were lucky you managed to get on the steamer, the hiss and smell of the steam being much more healthy than the oily stench of the petrol driven boats, which made you feel sick before you started, and often seemed to have a quantity of oily water slopping around the deck, which was rather worrying.

Rudyard had other entertainments, and a visit to Mr Horam's amusement arcade was a must, provided you had a few pennies left to spend. 'Spiv' Horam, as we affectionately called him, had a variety of slot machines, some of which were always out of order. They gobbled up your coppers, and no amount of banging and shaking would make them perform. And woe-betide you if you tilted them to get a better result, for Mr Horam would escort you away!

The station, with its large staff of men and boys, was always busy, particularly on high days and holidays, when the long excursion trains brought in visitors by the thousand, discharging passengers on to the extended platforms, where the tickets were often collected in a bucket at busy times. The railway which brought so much prosperity to Rudyard ran very close to the edge of the lake on the eastern side, so that you could almost reach out and touch the water. It was always an exciting trip along this line when, as boys, we would travel in a school party to the Test Match at Old Trafford, Manchester. This was in the days when schools were able to do this kind of thing. Now a party of boys in the closed world of a fast moving railway carriage can be a potential for trouble. Frequently trousers were seen flying through the window, like pennants. Sometimes, as if taking pity on the hungry fish, some unfortunate boy's packet of sandwiches would be hurled into the lake. And cunningly devised contests were held, to see who could spit, or, even worse, pee into the lake. Nobody ever succeeded, for, against the wind and the speed of the train, this was a practice fraught with danger. But of course, we could never be branded as vandals, for we never did any real damage!

As you will have noted, Nithsdale, much of the real spirit of Rudyard is bound up with the lake. It has been the venue for regattas and water sports. Sailing has always been very popular, the white sails weaving a pattern across the water, making an attractive picture against the wooded banks and the surrounding hills. Then in the winter, when the surface of the lake was frozen, it became a skaters'

Rudyard Lake - 'The Giant's Coffin' at the start of the canal feeder.

paradise, and once, in 1895, when sixteen weeks of frost created ice some 18 inches thick, the Leek Fire Brigade was able to drive over the frozen surface of the lake to attend a fire in a boathouse. Water always has a great fascination for people. Wherever there is a stretch of water - lake, pool, canal or river - there will always be someone to enjoy it, and for 200 years Rudyard Lake has provided leisure time activities for young and old.

I must tell you that Rudyard Lake is an artificial reservoir, dammed in a most exquisite valley, for supplying the local system of the Trent and Mersey canal. It was completed just over a hundred years ago, and has a claim upon the waters of the Dane from below Swythamley. A 'feeder' runs from thence through Rushton to the head of the lake by Rudyard Lake Station; and from the end the water is conveyed to the canal at Leek by the 'feeder' I mentioned as we walked to Rudyard.

As we leave Rudyard you cannot fail to notice the Jubilee Stone, standing like a silent sentinel at the junction of Lake Road and Whorrocks Bank - the local name for the Horton road. This stone obelisk was quarried from a local quarry just up the hill, and it is said that whilst being conveyed on its short journey downhill from the quarry it fell off the truck, and a large piece was broken off, leaving an irregular shape, the rough hewn repair being still visible today, standing like a giant's huge decayed tooth, as you enter or leave the village. The interesting feature of the Jubilee Stone is the vast number of important dates which are engraved on its dressed faces - royal events, national events, war and peace - a kind of potted history in stone of the past century. The inscription reads:

'Erected by the Parishioners of Horton in commemoration of the
Diamond Jubilee of Queen Victoria,
June 20th 1897'

You would remember the stone recording events just before your time, Nithsdale, but many more dates have been added since, including the Great War, which states 'began August 4th 1914, ended August 31st 1921', the Second World War and the Silver Jubilee of Queen Elizabeth II, June 7th 1977. The date of August 21st 1921 for the end of the First World War is perhaps puzzling for many, for the traditional date of the Armistice is November 11th, 1918. The reason for this is that, in 1921, a technical state of war still existed between America and Germany, and some American troops were still on the Rhine. On July 2nd 1921 President Harding signed a joint resolution of Congress declaring the war to be at an end, and claiming for the United States 'all rights, privileges, indemnities, reparations or advantages' to which it was entitled under the terms of the Armistice or the subsequent Treaty of Versailles. The following month the United States Government, through its Commissioner in Germany, signed in Berlin a separate treaty of peace with Germany - hence the date of 1921, the true end of the First World War! I am sure you are now the wiser, WH, for my explanation of this apparent anomaly, and with it we must now take our leave of Rudyard and its delights, and think of returning to Leek!

But before we do so, we will make one final diversion. As we follow the road out of the village, after passing under the railway bridge, we turn left into Green Lane. This joins the main Macclesfield road near to Freshwater. Now a trout farm, this was once the site of a popular open-air swimming pool, established in the 1930s by Harry Breaks, a local entrepreneur who, besides running stalls in Rudyard, also operated the splendid Bazaar in Stanley Street, Leek. After the austerity of the years of the Second World War and its aftermath, when people were finding more leisure time and enjoying greater affluence, Freshwater became a great attraction for the workers of Leek and Macclesfield. In some ways a mirror of the new permissive society, Freshwater provided a venue where shop girls and typists, secretaries and students, machinists and factory workers, in the briefest of the daring new style swimwear, put on a display of exposed flesh, which turned from lobster pink to fiery red under the summer sun. Now only the grey-brown trout glide silently in the peaceful waters. But Freshwater managed to put a little sparkle and a little glamour into many peoples' otherwise mundane lives, and deserves to be recognised, and perhaps mourned, as a greatly missed local amenity.

Memorial Stone, Rudyard, showing the panel commemorating the First World War

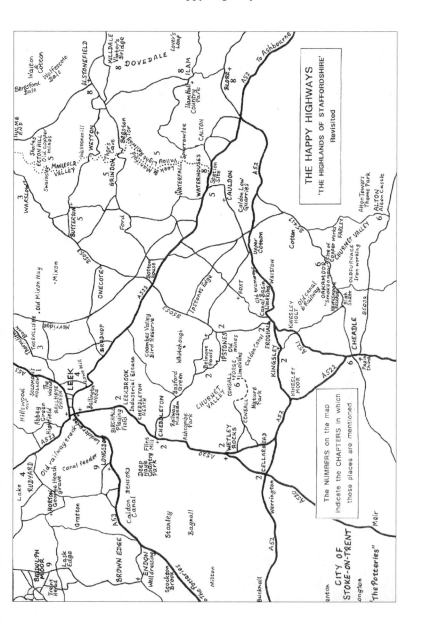

THE HAPPY HIGHWAYS
'THE HIGHLANDS OF STAFFORDSHIRE'
Revisited

The NUMBERS on the map
indicate the CHAPTERS in which
those places are mentioned

Cycle hire at Waterhouses station site - today's wheeled access to the Manifold Valley

CHAPTER V

THE VALLEY OF THE MANIFOLD
The Light Railway, Hulme End, Ecton, Wetton,
Grindon and Butterton

THIS IS ONE OUTING, WH, which you were certainly able to enjoy in a way which we cannot today, for you were able to travel along the Manifold Valley by the old Light Railway. The Leek and Manifold Valley Light Railway was a splendid creation, though doomed to failure from birth. Now it is not our business here to record a detailed history of this splendid little railway - this has already been done very ably by others - but a few historical facts are necessary in order to appreciate the story of the line and its impact on the countryside.

At the turn of the century this remote part of the Staffordshire Moorlands was not served by a railway. It was a largely agricultural area, with a thriving dairy industry and some quarrying and mining, with the possibility of re-opening the copper mines at Ecton. It seemed, therefore, that freight traffic was assured, and passenger and tourist traffic with day trippers would surely follow. The nearest railways were at Leek, Ashbourne and Buxton, and here, at the centre of the triangle, as it were, was an area desperately in need of a viable transport system. Fortunately, in spite of much opposition, there were enough local men of vision and enterprise to back the dream with cash.

The North Staffordshire Railway Company showed some reluctance, and a separate company was formed. The idea was to construct a standard gauge line from Leekbrook, just south of Leek, on the Churnet Valley Line, through Bradnop and Ipstones to Waterhouses, with a short branch to the quarries at Caldon Low. The Manifold line followed the valley from Waterhouses to Hulme End, some eight miles to the north. It was to be steam operated on a narrow gauge track, for this would make a saving of over £15,000. This was made possible under the provisions of the Light Railways Act of 1896. The stage was set, and the new company quickly applied itself to the task in hand. Enter the Indian connection, for the consultant engineer engaged by the company was E.R.Calthrop, who had great expertise in the construction of light railways, having worked as a locomotive inspector on the Great Indian Peninsular Railway. His theories had been put into practice in the construction of the Barsi Light Railway - some 200 miles of 2ft 6in gauge line, the very gauge that was to be used for the Manifold line. The resident engineer for the construction of the line was J.B.Earle, and these two men gave their names to the two splendid little locomotives which operated the line. It is interesting to note that the company was keen to extend the line through Longnor to Buxton, but this idea was never fulfilled.

Whit Monday, May 23rd 1904, was the date set for the opening day, but there were delays and the ceremonial opening did not take place until Monday, June 27th 1904. The Directors and other civic dignitaries assembled at Waterhouses, and the opening ceremony was performed by the Lord Lieutenant of Staffordshire, the Earl of Dartmouth. The occasion was vividly and effusively described in the Railway Magazine:

> ....on arrival at Waterhouses we found the little town en fête, gay with flags and banners, and arches of evergreens, while mottoes, more or less appropriate, were displayed at intervals. At the terminus of the light railway we found a train consisting of two carriages and two trucks provided with temporary seats. Lord Dartmouth having briefly declared the line open, the invited guests took their seats, and we started on what proved to be an exceedingly pleasant journey. We accomplished the run of $8^1/_2$ miles in 34 minutes, not an excessive speed, but sufficient for those who wished to enjoy the glorious scenery - now viewed by most of us for the first time - through which we passed. .... At Waterhouses luncheon was spread in a large marquee, and several hundred people, their appetites sharpened by the bracing air of the hills, heartily partook thereof. Congratulatory speeches were made by the Earl of Dartmouth, Mr Charles Bill MP, Sir Thomas Wardle, Colonel Boughey, a member of the Light Railway Commission, and other gentlemen.

This was the auspicious beginning of the short life of the Leek and Manifold Valley Light Railway, for it ran for a mere 30 years, until its closure in 1934. The reasons for the line's failure are many and varied. There is no village actually in the Manifold and Hamps valley - all the communities are outside the valley itself, so potential passengers in Waterfall, Butterton, Grindon, Warslow and Wetton had a long walk and a steep climb to get from the train to their homes. Freight traffic declined, and it was not a viable proposition to re-open the mines at Ecton. The creamery at Ecton, producing milk and cheese, gave some business to the line for a while, but this ceased in 1932.

It is said that in the days of the railway it was possible for a churn of milk to be loaded on a wagon in Ecton and stay on that same wagon until it reached the heart of London next day. This was made possible by means of the flat, low-bodied transporter wagons which operated on the line. The standard gauge trucks were carried on the transporters, from where the standard gauge line ended at Waterhouses right into the heart of the valley. Ingenuity and inventiveness were the hallmarks of the little railway. Its operators were very resourceful, and were usually able to find inventive ways round their problems. The little tea rooms along the line, though pretty basic by today's standards, were well patronised, and provided welcome refreshments for hikers and visitors. Not surprisingly, the line was often referred to as the 'Toy Railway'.

But perhaps the story of the little railway and its fate is best summed up by one anonymous local, who said that it would never do any good because it started from nowhere and went nowhere! Your own description, my friend, gives a good impression of what it was like to travel on this unique little railway:

We ran leisurely into the valley, the speed limit of these lilliputian trains being a respectable dozen miles an hour, and presently pulled up at the first station, Sparrowlee. And what a station! A platform flush with the rails, a sign post, and a seat; and one farmhouse a couple of hundred yards away........... Beyond Sparrowlee the line begins the bewildering winding in and out among the intricate maze of the Hamps, and our train started an elaborate game of bo-peep with the wooded hill sides, careering now to this and then to that bank of the narrow heights; and ever and anon, as it rounded a sharp curve, awakening the echoes with a not unmusical call from the flanges of tyres on the rails' sides. Then, as we ran further down the valley, with Soles Wood on the one hand........the valley opened wider and we were treated with glimpses of the higher peaks.

When the railway finally closed in 1934 the track was taken up, a hard surface was laid, and the trackbed became a route for walkers and cyclists. It quickly became very popular, for it opened up a whole area of magnificent countryside to the populace, and people flocked in by the hundred, on foot and cycle, to savour its delights. I well remember an old lay preacher who said that one Sunday he went for a ramble in the Manifold Valley and was shocked to see approaching him a group of 'cy-cyclists' as he called them, starting the word with a double syllable. 'Cy-cycling on the Sabbath day' seemed to him the ultimate sin, though why he considered it more evil than rambling on a Sunday I know not! However he qualified his feelings by saying that "some of the young ladies were wearing very short shorts!" Perhaps an example of a man with a narrow view but a wider vision?

My own first encounter with the Manifold Valley came at a very tender age. On a fine day we caught the early morning Ashbourne bus from Leek and got off at Waterhouses. We followed the valley northwards, passing the craggy face of Beeston Tor, to Thor's Cave where we climbed the steep path to the cavernous mouth and ate our ham and lettuce sandwiches. After waving to a group of 'cy-cyclists' we made our descent and started back for Waterhouses, and the bus home. But some mysterious force appeared to have lengthened the track since we walked that way in the morning! "How far now?" was my frequent, wearied cry, which would be met with the reply, "Not very far. When we get to Sparrowlee we shall be nearly there." "But where's Sparrowlee?" "Just round the next bend."However, there were a number of 'next bends' before we finally reached the end of the track, just in time to catch the bus home!

THOR'S CAVE IS AN AWESOME SIGHT. It has an air of mystery and magic, particularly if you see it on a dark and foggy day, when it looms through the mist like some ancient, fearsome beast, its cavernous mouth a petrified, grim snarl. This is how you described it:

*Thor's Cave, a large cavern in the face of a bleak and
forbidding majestic limestone cliff standing sentinel full four
hundred feet sheer above the river, the most impressive
spectacle along the whole length of this wonderful valley,
played hide-and-seek with us as we journeyed steadily up from
Weags........the stately magnificence of that gaunt, grey, black-
holed headland dedicated to the Scandinavian god of thunder,
showed itself now on our right and now on our left, while we in
our pigmy train approached its base.*

Thor's Cave, besides being a splendid tourist attraction and a
challenge to the walkers who make the steep ascent from the valley
to the cave's mouth, has excited the interest of archaeologists and
historians for many years. Neolithic, Bronze Age and Romano-
British relics have been found in the area, giving strong evidence of
the presence of early man, and adding to the mystery and romance of
the area.

Mystery and romance were the hallmarks of a local man who
made use of Thor's Cave for an unusual ceremony during the 1930s.
Ralph de Tunstall Sneyd was a member of the very influential Sneyd
dynasty - a local family of powerful landowners in the North
Staffordshire area in Victorian times. He was a highly individual
character with very wide interests. He was a Roman Catholic with a
deep understanding of most of the world's religions, including
Buddhism and theosophy. Something of a mystic, a burning driving
force in his life was his desire to search for the Holy Grail. Thus, he
called himself a Knight of the Round Table, and Arthurian Legends
gave him much inspiration for his poems, which he wrote
prolifically, and published in 1929. It was his Druid beliefs, however,
that led Ralph de Tunstall Sneyd to choose Thor's Cave as the setting
for the ancient and venerable Gorsedd Ceremony at midsummer,
when many Druids assembled on the site to re-enact the age-old
ritual. And what is more, he chartered the little Manifold train to
transport the party to the base of the cave. This, apart from the
opening day, was perhaps the most unique occasion in the life of the
line - a train-load of Druids travelling on the Toy Railway. The

Manifold Valley and Thor's Cave gave Ralph de Tunstall Sneyd the inspiration for one of his poems:

Midst the purple heather springing
Come the Hamps and Manifold;
Through the meadows verdure bringing,
Where the May-flowers gleam like gold;
Seeking haunts where birds are singing,
Wild abodes in mountains bold.

All around is woodland glory,
Where the wild rose loves to dwell;
Many a mighty cliff and hoary
Rises from the bosky dell;
Hermit saints of olden story,
In this place did worship well.

Once the baleful fire was gleaming,
In that cavern far on high
In yon mighty rock, and cauldrons
For the awful gods stood nigh;
Once the crimson blood was streaming;
And the pëon rose on high.

But, amidst the lonely mountains,
Where the shining waters go,
And where gleaming rivers vanish,
Sinking to the caves below;
There the sons of Christ contended
With the pagans long ago.

And even today, it is said, in the quiet calm of Midsummer's Eve, the sounds of the chanting of human voices can still be heard, drifting over the silent valley, making the campers in their tents at Wetton Mill feel, perhaps, just a little uneasy.

ECTON AND HULME END were out of reach to us as boys, Nithsdale - just too far to walk, and you had to wait until you got your first cycle to reach them. But the story of the copper mines at Ecton was well known to us, a moorland El Dorado, where untold riches might be found. This was certainly true for the Dukes of Devonshire, who successively owned the mines for many years, for it is said that the profits from one year's working was sufficient to build the impressive Crescent at Buxton. Mining was taking place as early as 1622, and it soon became apparent that at Ecton there was a rich supply of good quality copper ore. This was exploited by successive Dukes in the boom years of the 18th and early 19th centuries. Records suggest, however, that the Duke did not exploit his workers, indeed, quite the opposite, for he paid a fair wage, and working hours, though hard, were shorter than those in other industries and agriculture. Provision was made for health care and a school was provided for the children of the miners. The truck system under which workers were forced to buy their necessities from their employers was not used, and conditions were not as degrading as in the coal mining areas of the Potteries and the North of England.

But the work was hard. Let us try to imagine what it was like to work in the Ecton copper mines. You are working in the dark, in a very confined space, with only a flickering candle. The air that you breathe is fouled by the suffocating smell of sulphur. The temperature is so hot that you are working nearly naked, the sweat making the dust into a mud which cakes your body and runs into your eyes, and as you rub them you are blinded by the mixture of dust and sweat. You long for the fresh air and the sunshine but they are hundreds of feet above you, and down in this subterranean passage you are only aware of the rattling of wagons, the clash of pick and hammer and the constant boring and blasting of the rocks. Your own feelings about the mines, Nithsdale, was that they might have had some potential as a tourist attraction: ....

......there is an opening for an enterprising someone to show visitors through the old workings at so much a head. A charter from the railway company, and a small outlay in wax candles, would open up a little gold mine to a man sufficiently antiquated and voluble to assume the character of an old miner.

No gold mine, my friend, but the area attracts many tourists, walkers and cyclists, to this remote part of the lovely valley. Ecton Hill, which was once scarred and pitted by the extensive mining activities is green again; Nature has re-asserted itself. All who visit the Manifold Valley know this grand, windy hill with its smooth green sides and rounded summit, where you can walk on the lonely, bare mountainside.

Whatever the season of the year, Ecton Hill has its own appeal. In summer, under a blue and white windswept sky, you can look north and east over a spacious landscape, or west into the enchanting valley below. At other times the rain might lash at you almost horizontally up the valley, stinging like needles of ice. It is a different experience again to be there when the mist closes in, shutting the hillside away from the world, and you feel a strange remoteness, a loss of sense of time and place. And that gentle brush you felt on your shoulder - was it the cold branch of a bush, or did an old miner from a bygone age pass quietly by in the mist?

REFERENCE IS OFTEN MADE to the name of the River Manifold as being derived from the fact that, following a very meandering course, it was dubbed 'the river of many folds'. The Middle English word *manifeald* means manifold, of many parts, complex. The early English poet, Michael Drayton (1563-1631), wrote a great topographical poem on the land of England, which he called 'Poly-Olbion'. This was perhaps the first attempt to rouse the people of England to the beauties and grandeur of their countryside. His long poem covered a wide area, and he did not neglect North Staffordshire. An extract from 'Poly-Olbion' describes the Manifold as follows:

> ....Crankling Manyfold,
> The first that lends Dove force;
> of whose meandered ways
> And labyrinth-like turns (as in the moor she strays)
> She first received her name.

Unlike the Dove, the humble Manifold has not provided the inspiration for many poets and writers. We have sampled the work of Ralph de Tunstall Sneyd, and now I will quote you, Nithsdale:

To my mind the Manifold's chief claim to fame lies in the fact that, from below Wetton Mill to Ilam, it runs a double course. It lives a double life so to speak. The one, obvious: open to the heavens; making fertile the strip of adjoining meadow land, and serving as a watering for numerous cattle and sheep, as well as affording sport to disciples of Izaak Walton. The other hidden and subterranean, and in a dry season insidiously draining every drop of the precious water from the useful bed above; making life miserable for the farmer and his stock; surprising and driving away the unsuspecting camper-out; leaving the stepping-stones high and dry and for the time being superfluous, and here and there a pool - with imprisoned trout - which eventually becomes absorbed by evaporation.

As you observed, Nithsdale, the River Manifold is often referred to as the 'disappearing river'. Indeed, as we walk the old light railway track through the valley we pass many sections where the river is a dried up rocky bed with hardly a hint of water. The River Hamps, a tributary of the Manifold, behaves in much the same way. Its name possibly derives from a Middle English word which means the same as the word we know today as 'hamper', that is to say 'restrain, hold back, fetter or clog'. Thus, the flow of the stream is fettered, or held back in some way. In other words, a disappearing river. The reason for this is a strange phenomenon, often associated with limestone areas, where the water of the river disappears down sink holes, only to rise to the surface again further down its course. This is true of the Manifold, which disappears below Wetton Mill, to follow an underground course and eventually emerge through 'boil holes' in the grounds of Ilam Hall, at a spot appropriately known as Paradise.

LET US LEAVE THE VALLEY NOW, my friend, and explore the moorland above, with its villages that the little railway failed to serve. Grindon is an airy moorland village. The Anglo Saxon origin of its name - grene dun - literally means 'green hill'. The moorland countryside which surrounds the village is quite superb, as you discovered for youself,

Thence we crossed Grindon Moor, a moorland haunt of the pewit and a desolate region affirmed by superstitious farm folk to be traversed at night time by a headless rider; and turning to the right, we tramped down the hillside towards Hillsdale, enjoying meanwhile a grand view of the Ecton Hills.

The headless horseman seems to be an ubiquitous character in Moorlands folklore. There is the tale of an Onecote farmer who was on his way home from Leek market when he was suddenly scooped up onto the rider's horse, and after a hair-raising ride, leaping hedges and fences and ditches he was dumped on the ground at his home, battered, bruised and dazed. A few days later, it is said, he died. Others who have seen the apparition and survived have enlisted the help of clergymen to exorcise the demon rider. The only confession elicited was that the rider was an evil spirit cast out from Heaven and doomed to roam the earth until the final days. How the clergymen handled the situation is not known. Just as Windsor Forest had its Herne the Hunter and Kirk Alloway its Tam O'Shanter, so the Moorlands had the headless horseman!

MOORLAND WINTERS ARE NOTORIOUSLY SEVERE, as you well knew, Nithsdale. The old cliché about our local weather that we get nine months winter and three months bad weather is sometimes all too true. Moorland villagers are a hardy breed, and often have to endure the prospect of being cut off from the outside world for several days. With the wider use of transport, more advanced snow clearing methods and better forecasting these problems can usually be avoided.

But this was not so in 1947. This was probably the worst winter in living memory, with continuous snow for many days. Roads were closed, villages and farms cut off and transport thrown into utter chaos. Snow lay deep over the countryside, like a thick blanket. Hedgerows, walls and fences were buried, and in places you could walk on the drifts and touch the telephone lines. Schools were forced to close, giving children unlimited opportunity for sledging and snowballing. I was at school at the time, enduring your *endless hours of all manner of elementary monotony, from multiplication to the intricacies and irregularities of the verb 'to be'*, my friend, but I was denied these innocent pleasures. I was confined to home with an injured big toe, and could only watch the snow drift endlessly down, filling the streets and the gardens, and listening to the horrendous stories of events in the world outside. None were more appalling than the events which occurred on Grindon Moor on the morning of February 13th, 1947. Newspapers on the previous day carried reports of planes standing by, waiting to drop food to bring relief to North Staffordshire villages, some of which had been cut off for about a fortnight. Low cloud was a hazard, but a Halifax bomber set out on a mission to drop food for the Grindon area. There were six RAF crew members on board, with two press photographers. Tragically the aircraft crashed on the moors, and all eight on board were killed.

This tragedy had a profound effect on the moorland villagers, who have never forgotten the events of that fateful morning in 1947, and there is a permanent memorial in the church at Grindon. The story has a tragically ironic twist - the road to Grindon was cleared within a few hours, and food delivery vans were able to get through from Leek!

THE MOORLAND AROUND Wetton, Grindon and Butterton owes as much to Derbyshire as it does to Staffordshire. It is a country of stone walls rather than hedges. The green hills are criss-crossed by a higledy-pigledy pattern of walls, giving the landscape a chequered appearance. Old roads and trackways interlace them like threads in a gingham fabric. Farm gates break the pattern, in many cases, with a greater or lesser amount of decay, the old wooden gate has survived, usually the traditional five-barred type. They may be less efficient than the clinical new galvanised tubular steel variety, but they certainly have more character! The passage of humans is marked by moorland stiles, each one having its own particular character. Someone should make a study of moorland stiles, for they are as varied and individual as the village characters who gather round the bars in our country pubs. Sooner or later the old stone stiles will be replaced by the rather more stereotyped wooden ones, which our various local authorities, in their wisdom, seem to prefer. These are no doubt easier to negotiate, but are somewhat lacking in character. Shakespeare, in *As you like it*, says,

> Find tongues in trees, books in the running brooks,
> Sermons in stone, and good in everything.

You can certainly see our moorland stiles as 'sermons in stone', an eloquent though silent preaching on man's journey through life. Here will pass generations of children, on their way to and from school, here will come young lovers, hand in hand, to linger, leaning against the old stones. Across these fields, along pathways linked by stiles, have walked the old workmen, finding the shortest way home, tired after a day's labour, perhaps in the mines at Ecton, or in the hay field. Along this way has come the old verger, in his Sunday best and with his churchwarden's pipe, summoned by the bells, on his way to church. And maybe, perhaps, at the last, the old man with his dog, forcing his tired old limbs to carry him along the familiar pathways he has known since he was a child making his way to school.

Moorland stone stiles are usually of very great age, and come in many different forms. The narrow 'squeezer' stile, tapered towards the bottom, may well keep the sheep confined within the field, but are not welcomed by the corpulent hiker. Stiles with steps are often composed of stones worn smooth with the passage of many feet over the years. Sometimes you must go over the wall, and here the craftsmanship of the drystone-waller has ensured that large, flat stepping stones have been inserted firmly into the structure of the wall. Stiles can be complex, with three or more vertical stones placed in a staggered formation, so you pass through in a slalom-like formation. No two stiles are alike, and they stand like silent sentinels, a testimony to man's enduring imprint on the landscape.

SO, MY DEAR NITHSDALE, let us end this chapter where we began, with the light railway, and let us, in our imagination, return to Leek the way you did.

Half past seven found us again at Hulme End; ready for the hide-and-seek, the elaborate bo-peep, the echo-awakening tyre solo, the occasional engine shriek and continual smoke of the return journey. And punctually at nine o'clock we arrived in Leek, tired but thoroughly satisfied with our panoramic feast, and our day in the Valley of the Manifold.

CHAPTER VI

A-WHEEL AGAIN

Consall Forge, Consall, Cheadle, Oakamoor,
Alton, Farley, Cauldon Quarries and Windy Arbour

CHURNET COUNTRY AGAIN! The mid-Churnet Valley area is full of surprises, and yet again, like so many of the greener parts of the Staffordshire Moorlands, the area once had its industries, and if we read the signs in the landscape we find much evidence of these. Our excursion will take us to the heart of the Churnet Valley, where nature has now re-affirmed its claim to this green and pleasant land, after a productive industrial past. Now, in the springtime, in the valley's green heart, can be seen the wild flowers which Perdita speaks of in Shakespeare's *The Winter's Tale*:

> ....daffodils,
> That come before the swallow dares, and take
> The winds of March with beauty; violets dim,
> But sweeter than the lids of Juno's eyes
> Or Cytherea's breath; pale prime-roses,
> That die unmarried, ere they can behold
> Bright Phoebus in his strength.

The Caldon Canal and the Churnet Valley Railway form the threads through the valley along which our journey will be made.

Consall Forge, with its extensive but long disused limekilns, is a pretty waterside and railroad settlement. The Churnet is here discarded for the artificial waterway and, by the station, the river, rail and canal run practically side by side. Footpaths lead through the woods, which in their season are blue with forget-me-nots. The heights on either side, on the left to Belmont, and the right to Consall village, are each accessible by means of the "Devil's Staircases", long irregular stone steps set at some remote period, and thoughtfully assisted by a later authority with acceptable handrails.

Caldon Canal and Black Lion, in the heart of the Churnet Valley at Consall Forge

Consall Forge, my friend, is in the deep, green heart of the valley. Here something unusual happens to the river and canal. From Oakmeadow Ford Lock, just south of Cheddleton, in a narrow section of the valley, the canal builders utilised the River Churnet itself as the waterway, and river and canal share the same bed. At Consall Forge they divide and go their separate ways, the river following its natural course, to power water mills further down the valley, and the canal resuming its man-made route, close to the railway. Along this stretch of river-canal, near to a well-preserved old limekiln, two canal mile-posts, one stone and one iron, stand side by side, reflecting the story of the Caldon Canal. The older one, a block of rough-hewn stone, carries on its two flat faces, the mileage from Etruria to Froghall - the original extent of the canal. The newer one, a tall, silent, cast iron memorial to the canal age, shows the mileage between Etruria and Uttoxeter, a reminder that in the early years of the Nineteenth Century the canal was extended to Uttoxeter. This extension was short-lived, because the building of the railway in 1849 literally obliterated it.

There are many old limekilns in the Churnet Valley, and there is a fine, well-preserved bank of them at Consall Forge. Nearby, the flight of steps which you observed in your day, my friend, descends the steep slope into the valley. If you count these and then go back and count them again it is fairly certain that you will get a different answer. The Devil's Staircase exerts its own particular form of devilry. However, I can, with confidence, assure you, that at the last count there were 204.

Consall Forge, as its name suggests, was the site of a Seventeenth Century iron smelting forge. Robert Plot, in his 'Natural History of Staffordshire' (1686), describes it in his own inimitable style:

From the Furnaces, they bring their sows and pigs of Iron when broken afunder, and into lengths, to the Forges; which are of two forts, but commonly (as at Cunfall) ftanding together under the fame roof; one whereof they call the Finery, the other the Chafery: they are both of them open hearths, upon which they place great heaps of coal, which are blown by bellows like thofe of the Furnaces, and compreffed the fame way, but nothing near fo large. In thefe two forges they give the sow and piggs 5 feverall heats before they are perfectly wrought into barrs. Firft in the Finery they are melted down as thin as lead where the Metall in an hour thickens by degrees into a lump or mafs which they call a loop this they bring to the great Hammer raifed by the motion of a water wheel and firft beat into a thick fquare, which they call a half bloom. Then 2ly they put it into the Finery again for an hour, and then bring it again to the fame Hammer, where they work it into a bloom, which is a fquare barr in the middle, and two fquare knobs at the ends, one much lefs than the other, the fmaller being call'd the Acony end, and the greater the Mocket head. And this is all they doe at the Finery. Then 3. the Acony end is brought to the Chafery, where after it has been heated for a quarter of an hour, it is alfo brought to the Hammer, and there beat quite out to a bar, firft at that end; and after that, the Mocket head is brought alfo 4. to the chafery, which being thick, requires two heats, before it can be wrought under the Hammer, into bars of fuch fhapes and fizes as they think fitteft for sale. Whereof, thofe they intend to be cut into rodds, are carryed to the flitting Mills, where they firft break or cut them cold with the force of one of the Wheels into fhort lengths; they are put into a furnace to be heated red hot to a good height, and then brought fingly to the Rollers, by which they are drawn even, and to a greater length: after this another Workman takes them whilft hot and puts them through the Cutters, which are of divers fizes, and may be put on and off according to pleafure: then another lays them ftraight alfo whilst hot, and when cold binds them into faggots, and then they are fitting for sale.

Dr Plot, in his skilful way with words, has given us a graphic description of Seventeenth Century technology in non-technical terms. The meaning of the term 'pig iron' is clearly explained. Plot, the perfect eye-witness, describes exactly what he saw, and we get a picture of a hard working environment, with gangs of sweating labourers toiling in the extreme heat of the fiery mouth of the furnace. However, the work was well arranged, for they used the summer months for essential outside work - gathering a plentiful supply of the raw materials, ironstone from the local mines, charcoal from the surrounding woodland, clay for the lining and limestone for the flux. Then, in the autumn and winter, when the weather turned inclement and there would be a plentiful water supply, they would 'blow' the furnace, and the work would be centred on the one site, in the shelter of the furnace. Warm work indeed, for the cold winter months.

The poet, Edmund Blunden, in his poem entitled 'Forefathers', gives an picture of the rare breed of men who would work in these rural industries:

> These were men of pith and thew,
> Whom the city never called;
> Scarce could read or hold a quill,
> Built the barn, the forge, the mill.

Consall Forge is an isolated little community, bounded by the steep sides of the valley. It is approached by footpath, or the steep winding road, which vehicles delivering beer to the 'Black Lion' negotiate with great skill. In the early Nineteenth Century there was a little cluster of workers' cottages, and Methodism spread to the community. Meetings were held in one of the cottages, and the work prospered, enabling the society to acquire a plot of land on which they planned to build a chapel. However, the route of the Churnet Valley Railway in 1849 literally went right through the middle of the site, and the chapel was never built.

The surviving station building at Consall Forge is very unusual. It overhangs the canal, precariously balanced on iron cantilevers. Following the closure of the railway it fell into a ruinous state, and appeared about to collapse into the canal, when a rescue plan restored it to its former glory. It was necessary to construct it in this way so that railway and canal could co-exist in this narrow part of the valley, the overhanging station building allowing canal boats to pass under it.

A few yards further, opposite to a row of splendid former railway houses, stood one of the Churnet Valley's many water mills, Crowgutter Mill was a turbine-powered mill for grinding materials for the pottery industry. Its proximity to the canal gave it a ready facility for the transport of materials. The next bridge is known, perhaps somewhat incongruously, as 'London Bridge'. The use of the name of our capital city, heart of the nation's finances, is an indication of the importance of the valley's former industries of ironworking, quarrying, mining and milling.

Speaking of incongruity, there is another little oddity which, I suspect, eluded you, Nithsdale - but then, perhaps, it was not there when you took your trip into the Churnet Valley. If you follow the canal towpath to Consall Locks, and turn to cross the old railway line

Canal and railway bridge near Consall Forge

Consall station building, overhanging the Caldon canal at Consall Forge you will begin to ascend a steep and twisting path up Far Kingsley Banks, above Hazles Wood. Pausing to catch your breath halfway up the valley side you will be rewarded with a splendid view down the valley. Its wooded sides provided timber for the great wooden ships of Nelson's navy, and the charcoal for the iron forges. Its trees now give shelter to a wealth of woodland birds - woodpecker, thrush, woodcock, chaffinch, blackbird, crow, magpie, rook, starling and, in its season, the cuckoo. The view down the valley is spectacular, with the railway, river and canal snaking below, and the larger villages of Ipstones and Kingsley on either side of the valley tops. The path emerges on the lane to Kingsley village, near Hazles, where there is an odd sight. A finger-post points down into the valley, carrying the work of some unknown sign-writer whose error stands in perpetuity, for he tells us that the path leads to 'Consul Forge'. Perhaps he felt that the Roman legions passed this way!

NOW, MY FRIEND, WE WILL LEAVE THE VALLEY as you did, via Consall village, for we must make our visit to the town of Cheadle. Above the valley on the western side, Consall can be reached from Consall Forge either by climbing the 'Devil's Staircase', (don't forget to count the steps), or following the road by Consall Nature Park and Consall Hall. It is an interesting thought that the old Consall Plateway once climbed out of the valley here, following a more gentle course, curving up the steep slope. The ingenuity of the men who constructed these early industrial railways was a fine example of how to surmount seemingly insurmountable problems!

Consall, after a mile and a half of continual climb, we found to be a prettily situated cluster of farmhouses, one an exquisite example of half-timbered black and white architecture, some farm buildings and a few cottages. It has one other attribute, a well built but broken windowed deserted chapel, with an open door, and furniture fast falling to ruin.

Let me tell you, Nithsdale, a little story of the early Methodists at Consall, which illustrates the problems they frequently encountered. Meetings began in 1837, in a cottage home. One day the local gamekeeper, out of loyalty, told his master about the meetings.

The master, who was obviously more concerned about the fate of his game birds than the souls of the worshippers, felt that the meetings would attract all manner of loose and idle characters, including poachers, into the neighbourhood, and ordered that the meetings be stopped, or the tenant of the cottage would risk eviction. Meetings, however, continued surreptitiously, in spite of the threat, and the work prospered.

A mile along a pretty lane through fertile pasture lands brought us to the Cheadle highway, whence presently we emerged into Blakeley Lane, and shortly on the misnamed Kingsley Moor. Turning to the right at the first fork we ran down the dark surfaced and rather uninteresting road, by Parkhall colliery on the right and Harewood Park on the left, and about half-past eleven turned sharply to the right again into Cheadle High Street.

Cheadle, like Leek, is a market town, but its market place, just off the High Street, lacks the broad proportions of the market place at Leek. Nevertheless, on market days the compact area is crowded with stalls, and is well patronised. Like all markets, it attracts its own 'characters' in its stallholders and customers, and its character is enhanced by the row of Georgian properties at its rear, one of which once served as the tavern for the market. The seventeenth century market cross is well preserved, but, somewhat incongruously, this was 'adorned' in Victorian times with a gas street lamp! Cheadle's former industries included textiles, coal mining and brass and copper. The former Cheadle coalfield boasted the famous Crabtree seam - a coal of high quality. There were many small collieries in the area. The copper and brass industry came to Cheadle in 1719, when Thomas Patten of Warrington opened his works at Brookhouses.

One of the main textile factories was an extension of the large-scale Brough, Nicholson and Hall enterprise, which was based in Leek. To the north of Cheadle's High Street a complex of narrow streets and alleys rises steeply towards Cheadle Park, which overlooks the town. Passing the old Monkhouse School, at the foot of a steep hill, you climb to the site of the Cheadle water-works, for the town once boasted its own water supply, operated by a small staff, independent of the major water companies. This unique feature, of which the town was justly proud, is now part of a much larger water authority, and a little bit of individuality has been lost, presumably for ever. Looking down on the slate-grey, brick-brown town, with a sprinkling of Tudor black and white, you may well feel that all colour has been drained out of it.

Even the tall, slender spire of St Giles' Roman Catholic Church points heaven-wards like a lead pencil. From your vantage point you cannot see the richly-emblazoned great west doors, red with gold rampant lions. Nor can you appreciate the riot of colour and decoration which confronts you when you enter the church. You failed to note this splendid church when you visited Cheadle, Nithsdale, so we must make amends for your omission! Your first impressions of the church will immediately make you realise that you are witnessing a work of genius. That genius was the great Victorian architect, Augustus Welby Northmore Pugin. The Earl of Shrewsbury had commissioned Pugin to do some work at Alton Towers and Castle, and this association led Pugin into the project for a new Roman Catholic Church. The period of gestation was six years, from the conception and initial drawings in 1840 to the grand consecration ceremony in 1846. The Gothic Revival Movement was beginning to be a force to be reckoned with in Victorian architecture at the time, and Pugin was firmly in the van of it.

Nothing can prepare you for the astonishing sight which greets you when the lights in the church are switched on. Every inch of walls, floor, windows, pillars and ceiling is richly decorated. There are brightly coloured tiles by Minton and Wedgwood, important names in the pottery industry, and paintings by prominent Victorian artists. The use of tiles, stained glass, stone, alabaster, copper and oak, in the hands of a lesser genius, could well have been over-ostentatious. But Pugin has infused it with his own particular inspiration and flair, and has left, in this corner of the Staffordshire Moorlands, an example of his work which cannot be surpassed anywhere in the country.

The Parish Church at Cheadle is also dedicated to St Giles, and is the work of the Staffordshire architect, James Trubshawe. The churchyard has a memorial to Joseph Atkinson with a poem by a major literary figure, the poet Thomas Moore, who lived for a time

just outside the Staffordshire Moorlands, at Mayfield, near
Ashbourne. In a quality of verse superior to many graveyard
epitaphs, the poem begins as follows:

> If ever lot was prosperously cast,
> If ever life was like the lengthened flow
> Of some sweet music, sweetness to the last,
> 'Twas his who, mourned by many, sleeps below.

After extolling the virtues of the deceased, the poem concludes with
the words:

> All these were his: oh thou who read'st this stone,
> When for thyself, thy children, to the sky
> Thou humbly prayest, ask this boon alone,
> That ye like him may live, like him may die.

Cheadle itself is not without its poetical and literary
associations. Thomas Bakewell was a local man who worked in the
tape factory at Cheadle before setting up a private psychiatric
hospital at Oulton, near Stone. He wrote verse under the pen-name of
'The Moorland Bard', and his poetry, which some might dismiss as
doggerel, reveals a great sense of humour. In the early years of the
Nineteenth Century, Cheadle had a social club known as 'St.
Thomas's Club', the main qualification for membership being that
your Christian name must be Thomas. On a night when the club was
being held at the home of a certain Mrs Howe, the following incident
took place, described by Thomas Bakewell in this typical example of
his verse style:

> THE OYSTER EATERS DISAPPOINTED
> One ev'ning of late, when the Thomas's Club
> Were met to devour of oysters a tub,
> And all things prepar'd, knives, towel and ale,
> Nicely warmed and well ginger'd, our tastes to regale;
> Bread, butter, and vinegar, pepper - and now
> All completely made ready by the good Mrs.Howe.
> Friend Walters, whose strength you may tell by a look,
> Impatient for action, a hammer up took,
> And struck some hard blows with a direful intent;
> Then broke up the cover, and in his hand went.
> A pause now ensu'd, while he look'd very odd,
> Then exclaim'd Nought but shells and potatoes, by G-d!

> Dear reader, hadst seen that keen look of surprise,
> While stifled vexation, shot fire from all eyes:-
> But description would fail; so I leave thee to fill
> By fancy the scene, while I laugh till I'm ill.

Cheadle's Victorian historian was Robert Plant, whose 'History of Cheadle' was published in 1881. Plant wrote his history *'during moments snatched at intervals from the discharge of the active and not unfrequently embarrassing duties connected with the management of a large business concern.'* Samuel J. Looker was another Cheadle resident who broke into verse. A Twentieth Century poet, he wrote most of his verse between 1910 and 1950, finding his inspiration in the scenery of the Cheadle and Oakamoor area. His poems were published under the title 'Between the Churnet and the Dove - Poems of North Staffordshire. He became a devotee of the country writer Richard Jefferies, and wrote the introductory notes to a number of his books, for he was himself a lover of country life.

The name Masefield has a place of honour in the annals of English literature in the person of John Masefield, who became Poet Laureate in 1930. He was the cousin of a local naturalist, John Richard Beech Masefield, who founded Hawksmoor Nature Reserve, on the road from Cheadle to Oakamoor. The imposing entrance gates to Hawksmoor are a memorial to J.R.B. Masefield. They were officially dedicated to his cousin by John Masefield on 21st October 1933. A plaque commemorates the name of the founder in these words:

> He was a great naturalist with an unrivalled knowledge of the flora and fauna of his native county. For 49 years he was a member and four times president of the North Staffordshire Field Club, and was ever ready to help and encourage others in the study of natural history.

J.R.B.Masefield was the father of Charles Masefield, upon whom some of the literary talents of the late Poet Laureate had fallen. He was the author of a novel, 'Gilbert Hermer', which was set in the imaginary town of Cradleby - inspired by Cheadle! He also wrote the Staffordshire volume in the splendid 'Little Guides' series, published by Methuen in the Edwardian years. He wrote a few poems, but was tragically killed at Lens during the First World War, one of the many literary talents snuffed out in that great conflict.

NOW, MY GOOD FRIEND, we must return to the Churnet Valley, following the road from Cheadle to Oakamoor beside which the Hawksmoor Reserve stands. Before we reach there, however, we pass, at a sharp bend, a high point on the road. This is High Shutt, marked for many years by an ancient fir tree, and visible from the churches of Cheadle, Ipstones, Foxt and Kingsley. It is an open, lonely, windswept spot, a place of superstition. Macbeth's witches would not have been out of place on High Shutt. A tradition recalled by Robert Plant in his 'History of Cheadle' tells us that, if you walked around the tree a certain number of times, you were likely to hear strange sounds. The spot was avoided by the more superstitious, who believed that, after walking round the tree nine times, you would hear the sound of bells summoning you into the next world!

In the early Seventeenth Century the road from High Shutt to Cheadle was known as the Magna Via - the 'Great Road'. At that time the iron industry in the Churnet Valley was flourishing, and roads were needed for transportation. Booming industry creates more jobs, and in this case there was work for the road-makers and stone-cutters, as well as the carters and horsekeepers. From High Shutt the road descends into the valley, winding and twisting through some splendid mixed woodland, down to Oakamoor.

The Churnet Valley here is as fine, pictorially, as anywhere, but the village, which has grown along the valley and upon the hillsides, owes its prosperity to the copper tube and wire works, where the first Atlantic cable was made. These works seem animate with a desire to vitiate and darken the atmosphere, to which purpose the chimneys pour forth such dense volumes of black smoke as would in any town speedily bring the management into the police court, and justify the locality's local name of 'Smokeamoor'.

NOW LET ME TELL YOU, WH, that my first trip into this part of the valley was by the Churnet Valley Railway. It was a workmens' train, leaving Leek in the early morning, which seemed to be filled to capacity with crowds of men, with their lunch bags or boxes, travelling to work at Brittain's Paper Mill, Cheddleton, or Bolton's Copper Works at Froghall or Oakamoor. Thus, as we travelled south, the train gradually disgorged its passengers at different stops, until, after Oakamoor, we had the carriage to ourselves. We could then put up our feet on the seats, and contemplate the pictures on the carriage wall, by the luggage rack, usually a Bovril advert framed between two faded sepia photographs of holiday resorts, perhaps Llandudno or Lake Windermere. And why was the glass in the frame always cracked?

The station sign 'OAKAMOOR - ALIGHT FOR COTTON COLLEGE' prompted us to wind down the window and say to the guard on the platform, with the panache that only schoolboys can muster, "What's that for? Are they in the dark?" - a remark not made until the train was safely on the move! But, in spite of the workmen, this always seemed a rather more sedate train than the ones going north. We might sing the occasional song - 'Colonel Bogey', for instance, with our own words. But no trousers were flown through the window here - perhaps the countryside was too genteel, and we had to at least appear to be well-mannered, even if we were not!

THE CANAL AGE MADE ITS MARK on the Oakamoor area. The Caldon Canal to Froghall was proving to be a success in the late Eighteenth Century, and the proprietors had the idea of extending the canal from Froghall to Uttoxeter. The extension was authorised by Act of Parliament in 1797, and John Rennie was appointed engineer for the project. Rennie would be spending a lot of time in the area during those years leading to the turn of the century, for he was also working on Rudyard Lake, and later constructed the 1802 tramway from Froghall to Cauldon Lowe. There was fierce opposition from water mills in the area, who were concerned about water rights, and the construction of the new canal was greatly delayed. The Earl of Shrewsbury and the Cheadle Brass Company also raised objections, and after a long period of dispute the canal company agreed to raise and maintain the level of the weir at Alton Mill, thus ensuring a plentiful supply of water, but the work was not completed until 1811.

The 'Staffordshire Advertiser' of 14th September 1811 carried a graphic account of the ceremonies which marked the opening. Crowds turned out along the route, the cotton works at Rocester allowed its workers time off to see the events, there were lavish refreshments at various points and specially-written songs were performed - clearly it was a memorable occasion! And what happened to the canal? Sadly, it had only a very short life, for a mere 38 years or so later the Churnet Valley Railway was opened through to Uttoxeter in 1849. The railway literally obliterated the canal, and there are very few visible remains. However, as you follow the old railway track from Oakamoor to Alton there are a number of points where you can see evidence of the old canal - here a section still holding dark, muddy water, there a dry cutting filled with reeds, the occasional bridge, and the massive California Lock, with its coal wharf.

We can fully appreciate this part of the valley, my friend, as we walk the old railway track southwards from Oakamoor. The railway journey which first brought me to Oakamoor was a school excursion to Thomas Bolton's copper works. It seemed natural, and perhaps desirable, in those days for schoolboys to visit engineering works as part of their education, so Bolton's factories at Froghall or Oakamoor, or sometimes, if we were really lucky, the railway works at Crewe were our great engineering destinations. These school outings were a splendid treat, and were clearly meant to introduce us to the world of work. However, away from the disciplined confines of the school walls, they frequently turned out to be an excuse for extra-curricular activity that was rather less than educational. If you arrived at Leek station in the early morning, after the deliveries of fish had been unloaded, you could do all manner of unmentionable things with the odd fish that might have fallen out of the crates. And woe betide you if you opened the carriage window in Leekbrook tunnel!

The copper works closed a number of years ago, and, as with other former industrialized parts of the Churnet Valley, nature has reasserted itself, and the area is now a picnic site, with only a few immense concrete blocks and solid gate-posts to remind us of the works that used to dominate the area. As you leave the factory site you pass a row of old cottages, each with its tidy, small garden, somewhat incongruously named 'The Island'. This little community is, in effect, on an island between the river and the old mill-race on the one side, and the old canal on the other. But it was also, in the days of the copper works, almost an 'island' surrounded by the factory. At the site of the old station you can still see where the railway lines branched off into the sidings within the copper works, for rail traffic was carried right into the heart of the factory. Here, at the signal-box for Bolton's Sidings, Bob, 'Peg-leg' Johnson worked as signalman for a number of years, after losing both legs in a railway accident.

Beyond the old station site the valley has yet another surprise. Tucked into the bed of the valley is a delightful and well-appointed cricket ground, where Bolton's works team played its local league matches. Surrounded by the tree-lined sides of the valley, this is a perfect, peaceful setting for the summer game, and is another of the many fine, picturesque grounds with which the Staffordshire Moorlands is blessed. Oakamoor has another cricket ground at the top of the steep hill on the road to Cheadle, over 200 feet higher. There cannot be many places in the country where there are two cricket grounds at such a different height but separated by a mere half mile or so.

This part of the Churnet Valley, between Oakamoor and Alton, is peaceful and idyllic. But on summer days, WH, when the wind is in the right direction, you will be surprised to hear, drifting across the valley, the shouts and screams of people being entertained at the nearby Alton Towers amusement park, now a major tourist attraction in the Staffordshire Moorlands. It was not always so, however. John Heywood's illustrated guide of 1899, price one penny, had an advertisement which described Alton Towers as 'the Paradise of England'. The guide described the area in glowing terms:

It would be quite easy to spend a thoroughly delightful day in this charming neighbourhood, even if no such place as Alton Towers were in existence. The scene as you emerge from the station is picturesque to a degree; and it is more than probable that - without the present supreme attraction of the Towers - Alton and its district must have found its thousands of admirers among the hosts who now, summer after summer, rush from our smoky and noisy manufacturing towns in search of fresh air, and the quiet delights of hill and valley, tree and cliff, and river scenery. As it is with the glorious grounds and gardens of the Towers, which by the enlightened generosity of the Earl of Shrewsbury are freely thrown open to the public all the year round, there isnothing to wonder at in the fact that year by year the numbers of appreciative

visitors are largely increasing...........and throughout the season there is a
continuous stream of excursionists and visiting parties.

These inexpensive old guides were very popular in your day
and are charming, even if their language is rather flowery and
flamboyant. Their anonymous authors will never find a place in the
records of English literature, but we should be grateful for their
detailed descriptions.

One of the greatest legacies of the Earl of Shrewsbury are the
gardens at Alton Towers, enhanced by temples, fountains, grottoes,
conservatories, terraces, statuary and rockeries, all described by our
anonymous friend as 'a kind of earthly paradise'. The spirit of the
place, and the joy which the gardens gave to the Earl, is perfectly
conveyed in the poem which you discovered, my friend:

> A visitor once viewed with admiring delight
>   Famed Alton's fair landscapes and bowers,
> A scene of enchantment it seemed to his sight,
>   And he wondered who lived at the Towers.
> The question he put to a gardener near,
>   Who thought the enquirer half-witted
> "Why 'tis Shrewsbury's Earl." "Indade," the wight sighs,
>   And his brow he thoughtfully knitted,
> Then says: "If to heaven th' Earl goes when he dies
>   Do you think he'll know tha' 'ee's flitted?"

I suspect, my friend, with all the changes you see today at Alton
Towers, he would certainly know now!

YOUR RETURN TO LEEK, WH, took place in a violent
thunderstorm, which gave you a good taste of the fickle nature of the
Moorlands weather. You travelled through the once-quiet village of
Farley, and took the Ashbourne road to Cauldon Lowe. The road
from Cauldon Lowe to Waterhouses passes the Yew Tree Inn, which
is well worth a visit - and a good place to shelter from a
thunderstorm! Entering this old pub through its weatherbeaten door
is like entering a time capsule. And yet time is an important factor in
the scene which confronts you, for you will see an assortment of
antique timepieces which would make any collector envious. The
juke box and fruit machine have no place at the Yew Tree, but here
are their predecessors in abundance. Mechanical music making

Canada geese, Tittesworth

machines abound, all wonderfully in working order, so that the strains of the old music hall songs and choruses come tinkling through, as you enjoy your pint. Domestic and agricultural articles, tools and implements adorn the walls and hang from the low ceiling in this living museum of yesteryear, where the welcome is always warm and the atmosphere convivial. The pub where time stands still.

Time does not stand still at the vast quarries of Cauldon Lowe, where the 'inexhaustible supply of limestone' which the proprietors of the Caldon Canal claimed over 200 years ago is still being quarried. No longer is it transported down to Froghall Wharf, clattering down the tramways. No longer is it loaded into railway wagons at Waterhouses. Today road transport is used, and heavily laden lorries carry the stone away, a far cry from the Canal Age.

Caves are a feature of limestone areas, and Cauldon Lowe is no exception. A North Staffordshire Railway postcard of about 1910 shows the interior of a cave that was discovered during quarrying operations. The cave was 30 feet wide, 100 feet high and penetrated about 140 feet into the hillside. The postcard suggests that the whole of the cavity was an underground watercourse. The cave attracted a lot of attention at the time, but subsequent quarrying activities have now obliterated all trace of it.

SINCE WE ARE SHARING THE PLEASURES of your original outings, WH, it seems only fair that we should also share your discomforts. The violent thunderstorm which accompanied your return to Leek along the Ashbourne road, through Winkhill, Bottomhouse and Bradnop was a spectacular, if uncomfortable, experience - but at least our roads today are better surfaced.

The setting sun smiled upon our discomfiture as we raced through the mud down the long bank to New Street above Winkhill. Turning into the Leek and Ashbourne road we continued up by Berkhamsytch to Bottomhouse through the thick mud; along the level, then down the steady incline to the steep drop into Cook's Hollow through thicker mud. In fact it was mud all the way through Bradnop, and even thicker still as we turned the corner in the hollow for Lowe Hill. We made quick pace, however, and lighting-up time found us at home enjoying the comfort of welcome dry clothes.

Moorland walls and moorland geese

CHAPTER VII

ROUND THE ROCHES

By Tittesworth Lake, Ludchurch and Meerbrook

IT WAS A GOLDEN MORNING. Easter came a little late that year, so that by mid April the sun had gained some strength, and the air was warm and calm. My father had decided that, if the weather were fine on the morning of Easter Monday, we would set out for our first big walk of the season. Our destination was the Roches and Ludchurch, and I did not realise at the time, when I was but a lad, that we would be following your route to the Roches, WH, and on foot, for this is by far the best way to see this part of the Staffordshire Moorlands. Your starting point, like ours, was that part of Leek known as Ball Haye Green.

Ball Haye Green, Leek's only suburb and locally "Bawly Green", conjured in my mind a stylish residential quarter, but its plain brick cottages and tout ensemble like nothing so much as a mining village, disappointed me.

You were rather disparaging there, WH, of the area where I was born and grew up. Ball Haye Green is now very much a part of Leek; the town has grown around it. But in your day, my friend, and in my youth, it was almost separate from the town. The Haregate housing estate was developing over the area of once green fields, and the old part of Ball Haye Green stood almost like a frontier post. Indeed, in those days Ball Haye Green was often referred to as 'The Island'. Some even went so far as to say 'Cannibal Island', and that you needed a passport to enter! The walk from the town, following Ball Haye Road was a daunting experience for many, for the road passed the fringe of Ball Haye Wood, near the hall, and this was reputedly haunted by the ghost of 'Ball Haye Jack'. However, this did not deter us from our woodland adventures as lads, nor did it deter the American soldiers billeted at the nearby Ball Haye Hall from their rather more amorous adventures during the war years!

The natives themselves, the 'Islanders', were quite friendly, however, and there was a great community spirit in the area, filled out with characters who were larger than life, a Falstaff, a Pistol, a Mistress Quickly, Ford or Page around every corner. There was the old man from the house opposite to ours in Nelson Street, who had what can only be described as a backyard farm behind his house, where he kept chickens and hens, and even a pig. There was a stable at the rear, and a little dairy where he made ice cream. He would set out each day in his pony and cart selling his ice cream, which was called 'Okey-pokey' by the locals. If I happened to be out in the street when he returned home he would sometimes give me an ice cream if he had any left over, but it was usually melted by then, his ice having thawed during the day. The garden at the rear was wild and unkempt, and it was the Sherwood Forest for my Robin Hood. Here the great sword fight between Errol Flynn and Basil Rathbone was frequently re-enacted.

In the late 1930s the old Leek Silk Twist factory, which stood at the end of Nelson Street, burned down in an awesome fire. It was said that my friend the ice cream man was heard to comment, in somewhat vernacular language, that his old pig could have put out the fire quicker than the Leek firemen! I remember, in the days following the fire, seeing my grandfather, who had worked at the mill as a general factotum, sitting on an upturned box in what remained of his beloved boiler-house, surrounded by a scene of total destruction, smoking his pipe, and commenting philosophically, "Well, they've made a bugger of it now!" My grandfather was one of the old Ball Haye Green characters, but there were others. There was a solitary man who sold watercress from door to door. There were allotment gardeners and pigeon fanciers, who seemed to spend their days and nights at their lofts or in their gardens, which I found very dull and boring. I could never understand how they found so much pleasure in taking a crate of pigeons miles away, releasing them, and sitting by their lofts for hours and hours, eyes turned skywards, waiting for the birds to come home.

There was an old retired farmer, who always seemed able to produce a rabbit or hare on demand, like a conjurer out of a hat. There was a tiny, mild little man who worked in the mill and lived with his unmarried 'sister' who was huge, and kept him firmly under her ample bosom. (We could never understand why their surnames were different.) There were rogues and scoundrels, wife-beaters and womanisers, strumpets, drunkards and gamblers, and some who would not wish to see the police too often. There was the old barber who cut hair and shaved in his front room and was never short of a group of old men to talk of many things, and sort out the world and its problems, as well as providing a family planning service. There was the old couple at the Pie Shop, who made meat and potato pies in a dusty, floury, smoke-filled little shop, with a scrubbed, wooden counter, which today would be closed down on health grounds, but which, I think, never did anyone any harm. My grandfather's verdict on the pies, however, was that they were "more bloody 'tater than meat!" And, of course, there was the little shop that sold literally everything - knicker elastic that was useful for catapults, paraffin for making the odd fire, and dried peas for shooting through pea-shooters. We could buy string, chalk, nails and pins, which would have a variety of uses, and ink for soaking blotting paper pellets. There was candle wax for rubbing on doorsteps, and rope for tying door handles together. There was boot polish for blacking faces, and sherbet powder and liquorice for mixing with lemonade. And you could always find skipping ropes, balls and tops and whips for the more legitimate, if less entertaining, games and pastimes. Open all hours, it was a veritable cornucopia of a shop, a treasure house for children, and a provider of the solution to many a household problem, cooking, washing or cleaning. Ball Haye Green in those days was a very self-contained, almost insular, little community. School, chapel, shops and pubs were all on hand. It saw itself as quite separate from the main town of Leek, and valued its self-created independence. People did not speak of 'going down to the town', rather they would say that they were 'going to Leek', which was almost like making a journey to a separate town.

This independence is also reflected in the fact that Ball Haye Green has its own war memorial. Forming an arched entrance to the recreation ground, it records the names of all the men from the area who served in the First World War. It stands as a testimony to the real community spirit, by no means insular, which has always existed at Ball Haye Green.

BUT LET US RETURN TO OUR RAMBLE, Nithsdale, for the sun is up, and the open country awaits us. When I first did this walk with my father many years ago it was on a morning when the world seemed to have suddenly come awake after a dark winter. I can remember a world that had become green and white and yellow overnight, with new grass and leaves, blossom and spring flowers that became so vividly apparent as we left your 'plain brick cottages' behind, and walked through the fields below Wardle Barn Farm down to the old stone bridge. The stone bridge was another Mecca for children. Here we could splash in the river, lark around, swing from the low branches of the overhanging trees, and catch newts, frogs and bullheads, which we called 'bull-yeds', and do all manner of things you wouldn't want your father to know about. Today, however, my father and I strode past the spot, for I was on my very best behaviour. We pushed on up the track, passing Belfield's Rough, where at the end of the summer we would come to pick the biggest, blackest, juiciest blackberries around.

The track follows an open route above the west bank of Tittesworth Reservoir, passing South Hillswood and North Hillswood farms, with panoramic views stretching from the jagged skyline of the Roches to the clean ridge of Morridge, breasting the sky. We emerge on the Meerbrook road and proceed to the large field which we used to know as 'Big Bent'. This was the field where you could gather the biggest, tastiest mushrooms you could ever wish to find, which ran delicious black juice as they sizzled in the pan - perfect with oatcakes. Our mushrooming always had a competitive edge to it. You had to be up early to get the best crop, and it was always with a feeling of triumph that we saw other gatherers following in our wake. I remember turning over a crusty cow pat with the toe of my boot and finding under it the most perfect huge mushroom I ever found. Being incubated, as it were, by the rich, warm muck it had grown to immense proportions, and proved to be very savoury indeed! There was often someone, however, who had got there first, usually one of the old Ball Haye Green personalities. You could sit on a stile, waiting for dawn to break, only to find yourself following someone who had already gathered the lot! An old man once told me that one day he was there as dawn was breaking, and saw the mushrooms growing before his very eyes. "They were popping up all around me. It was just as though somebody were pumping them up with a bicycle pump." They were good tellers of tales and spinners of yarns, these old Ball Haye Green characters. Perhaps, though, he dispensed a little of Prospero's magic in Shakespeare's 'The Tempest', as one who:

> By moonshine do the green sour ringlets make,
> Whereof the ewe not bites, and you whose pastime
> Is to make midnight mushrooms.......

They seemed to claim a freedom to roam anywhere in the countryside, and were not restricted to footpaths. And if you were challenged by the farmer, saying, "Where do you think you're going?" you could always reply, "I'm just going back, sir!"

WE PASS THROUGH MEERBROOK, with its Norman Shaw church, old village school and post office. Often referred to in the local dialect as 'Marbruck', it is a scattered community of farms and crofts, with a cluster of substantial village cottages around the road junction, near the inn, which you would know as the Three Horse Shoes, my friend, but has now been re-named the Lazy Trout, in deference to the fishermen who find much sport in the nearby reservoir. The re-naming of pubs is a trend today, and some of the slick new titles are not always an improvement. There was another inn at Meerbrook, the Fountain, which disappeared when Tittesworth Reservoir was enlarged in the early 1960s.

The simple, unadorned Methodist Chapel stands close to the road. as you approach the lake. When the reservoir was enlarged, the road level had to be raised, and the wide grass verges now provide a vantage point for birdwatchers, for the lake is rich in bird life. Canada geese, mallard, coot and moorhens are among the more common to be seen, but the osprey has been an occasional visitor, causing a great stir of interest, and an influx of visitors who crowd in with their binoculars.

Leaving the lake on our left, the path lay through Lower Tittesworth Farm, then a small wood, again by another farm, and across fields to the road between Blackshaw Moor and Meerbrook. Following the road for a space we crossed the

Churnet ford, over which a bridge is badly needed, and took the footpath through the fields at Middle Hulme ...... Touching Upperhulme on our right we came into the road under Hen or End Cloud, which runs thence, at an altitude of one thousand feet above sea level, beneath the Roches. Words almost fail to describe the grandeur of the surrounding landscape with the heather-clad hillside and towering bleak rocks above us; a panorama away to Leek on our left, and an even finer one over Leekfrith and Gun to the Cloud, and then stretching along the high ridge of the far away horizon across Swythamley towards Shuttlingslow.

And so it is. We have reached the high road which runs beneath the towering, craggy rocks above us. A dark, forbidding house broods over Upperhulme, like something out of a Brontë story. This is Roche House, stone-grey and merging into the gritstone rocks which surround it, so that it almost becomes a part of this timeless landscape by avoiding contact with the Twentieth Century. Another, much smaller, dwelling which is literally part of the landscape, for it is built into the rock face, is Rock Hall. Until a few years ago this was the home of one of the Moorlands' unique characters. Self-styled 'Lord of the Roches' to the media, who loved to publish stories about his activities, 'Mr.Moller' to the local authorities, with whom he had the occasional brush, and 'Doug' to his many friends in the genuine climbing fraternity, lived with his wife in this simple homestead for many years. Here he endured many severe winters, burning wood to keep warm, and melting ice for water, for the house lacked mains services. Here in summer life became easier, but he was often the victim of those who did not respect his privacy, or obey the laws of the Country Code. He always welcomed sincere walkers and climbers, however, saying, "If they're right with me, I'll be right with them," which seemed a fair bargain. Doug knew these rocks like the back of his hand, and he had an intimate appreciation of the wildlife. He had many sightings of the wallabies then living in the area. A genuine eccentric, Doug and his wife were re-housed in a more modern dwelling a few years ago, and Rock Hall became a base for climbers, dedicated to the memory of Don Whillans, the famous mountaineer who died on Everest.

The Don Whillans Memorial Hut (formerly Rock Hall), The Roches

A FLIGHT OF STEPS cut into the rock face near to Rock Hall brings you to the somewhat unexpected sight of the Queen's Chair. An engraved plaque recalls a Royal event which took place locally on August 23rd 1872, when the Duke and Duchess of Teck visited Leek and Swythamley. The Duchess was cousin to Queen Victoria, and carried the title of Princess Mary of Cambridge. Later, as Queen Mary, she became the mother of Edward VII and George VI. The picnic on the Roches was a grand occasion, with all the local and county civic dignitaries and gentry present. Sir Philip Brocklehurst, whose home was Swythamley Hall, played a prominent part, and the Roches, being part of the Swythamley Estate, provided a spectacular setting for the Royal picnic.

We must now return to the road, my friend, for the moorland tracks await us. Walking this road with my father many years ago we were astonished to make the acquaintance of an enormous, hairy yak, which came lumbering towards us through the heather and bracken. He appeared to be quite friendly, and eyed us with some disdain, as if we were invading his domain, instead of the other way round, for these beasts rightly belong in Tibet. Clearly he was a survivor, along with the wallabies, of the private 'zoo' of foreign animals brought back to England by Sir Philip Brocklehurst from his world travels. However, we did not see a wallaby, for they are very shy of humans, and sightings are rare. There have been many occasions when a would-be wallaby-watcher has spent hours crouching motionless in the heather, only to be rewarded with stiff knees and a damp seat to his trousers! Sadly, they now appear to be extinct.

The road we are following eventually becomes gated, and I remember as father and I walked this way we came to a rather ramshackle wooden gate across the road. Crudely painted in whitewash on the gate was the message: PLEASE SHUT COW GATE. FAST IT TIGHT. This prompts some thoughts about the wonders of the English language, for this is the raw material with which Shakespeare, Milton and Tennyson weaved their glorious, soaring phrases. And here some simple, unknown local farmer had taken that same raw material and used it in his own rough-hewn, ungrammatical way to get his message across. Seven simple, uncomplicated words, strung together in a manner that was clear,

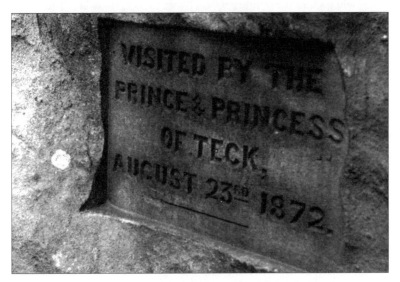

Stone panel commemorating the royal visit to the Roches.

precise and polite, leaving you in no possible doubt about what he wanted to say - and not a wasted word! Politicians, journalists and public speakers (and writers) would do well to note this.

At Roche End we leave the road and continue ahead, descending a rocky path through the bilberries, gorse, bracken and heather down to the dark edge of Back Forest. The sudden chill gives you the feeling that you are in a place of legends, and so it is. You may well now feel that you should have heeded the distinctive call of the grouse, bidding you to 'Go-back, go-back, go-back'. Miss Dakeyne, in her little book 'Legends of the Moorland and Forest', published in 1860, tells in verse the story of a tall, Robin Hood-like figure known as 'The Chieftain' who reputedly roamed the area in bygone days. The story runs along the familiar lines of legend. The Chieftain, in reality a nobleman who had been betrayed by a kinsman, accused of treachery and deprived of his lands and rights, becomes an outlaw and leads a band of rebels in the forest. He comes to his final confrontation with his betrayer, in the person of a huntsman, and a duel to resolve their differences is about to take place, when there is an intervention by an evil, ugly dwarf. The dwarf has his own reasons for wanting the death of the Chieftain, and aims a poisoned arrow at his heart. The huntsman intervenes, and takes the poisoned arrow in his arm. The chieftain then saves the life of his kinsman by drawing out the poison, is restored to his rightful place, goes off on a crusade to the Holy Land, where he finally dies an honourable death. The story weaves in many local references - Ludchurch, Back Forest, Swythamley and the church at Rushton Spencer.

> Not far from hence an ancient Castle stood,
> With quaint old Chapel in its neighbourhood;
> And, differently diverging, far away,
> Lie two broad roads, still called the Earl's Highway.
> Within that Chapel small there lay of old
> A form in armour, of a warrior bold,
> Of giant-like proportions; said to be
> Placed by his friend, Sir Swithelm of the Ley:
> His arms were folded close across his breast,
> And thus, 'twas said, the Chieftain sank to rest.

Ludchurch abounds in legends, including an Arthurian tradition. Its geographical location and physical description conforms to the circumstances of the meeting of Sir Gawain with the Green Knight. The Green Chapel is a perfect description of Ludchurch, and a modernised translation of the ancient tale says:

> But banks high and abrupt upon both halves
> And rough, knuckled outcrops with gnarled stones -
> He thought the very sky scraped by their peaks.........
> Then he bows towards the barrow, about it he walks,
> Debating with himself what it might be:
> It had a hole on the end and on either side,
> Was overgrown with grass in glades haywire,
> And all was hollow within, nothing but an old cave,
> Or a crevice of an old crag.

Such traditions are deeply embedded in our past, and colour the history of the local area. The Moorlands, indeed, any area, would be rather drab and colourless without a bit of magic and mystery. Ludchurch was reputed to be the secret meeting place of a group of Lollards - a Non-conformist religious sect in the 15th century, led by John Wycliffe. They were outlawed by the established church, and were surprised during their worship by a group of soldiers searching the moors for them. In the ensuing confrontation Alice de-Lud-Auk, daughter of the group's leader, was reputedly killed by a soldier's arrow. The unfortunate Alice, it is said, was buried at the entrance to the cleft.

We cannot leave Ludchurch and its legends without describing it, for although it is often written about, the emphasis is usually on the stories and not on the physical appearance and unique ambience of the place. You saw it, my friend, as a *'rocky fern-grown glen'* and a *'shady retreat, with its unexplored cavern, its ancient altar and halo of romance'*, and so it is. It cannot be seen from a distance; it is well hidden from view in the wooded hillside, where the land falls steeply through the dense undergrowth of bracken and bilberry to the infant River Dane bubbling over its rocky bed far below. The well trodden path, which generations of hikers have tramped, follows the terraced contour of the valley side, and it is easy to miss the entrance to Ludchurch, for it hides from the world, as if wishing to keep its secrets to itself. Walkers unfamiliar with the area can often be seen walking backwards and forwards along this section of the path, looking puzzled, and asking "Where is it?"

But you have to divert from the path to enter Ludchurch, for the fissure is at right angles to the valley. A short, narrow, overgrown section leads off the footpath, a modest entrance which does nothing to prepare you for the dramatic sight which greets you as the tremendous cleft opens up before you. A marked drop in temperature brings a sudden chill, and heightens the drama, for even on the hottest summer days it is cool in the cavernous cleft. The walls of sheer rock rise above you, seeming to close in around you, giving a distinct feeling of claustrophobia. The rocky floor, worn smooth by the passage of many walking boots, is treacherously damp and slippery. Mosses and lichens cling to the rocks, and shrubs grow precariously from crevices in the rock faces. You can walk through the cleft, which rises gradually towards the far end, where the steps cut into the stones lead you to the little patch of sky, to emerge on the open moor. A grand place, and one of the most delectable spots in the Moorlands, as you yourself testified, Nithsdale:

We continued along the rough road over the moorland, delighted with the charming views across the Dane Valley ..... We topped the crest of the ridge, and involuntarily stopped to admire the beautiful prospect across country to Gun Hill before us. It was magnificent! .... A liberal mile along the cart track brought us to Clough Head, where in a countryside rich in panorama and possessing a network of farm lanes and footpaths, we chose a deep rutted road beside briar bushes and gorse leading to the one running under the Roches.

This, my friend, was where we encountered our yak on the morning of our Easter hike, so we are on course to descend to Meerbrook, and retrace our steps to Ball Haye Green. Our bread and cheese sandwiches long consumed, the spread of tea awaiting us as Father and I arrived home was welcome indeed. Next weekend it would be cricket, and the first match of the new season!

ON SUNDAY EVENING, my friend, you paid a visit to Abbey Green, with some reflections on Dieulacres Abbey. Our story would not be complete without a few thoughts on this major influence on the early history of Leek. Founded in 1214 by the Earl of Chester, the abbey was of the Cistercian order, and was transferred from Poulton in Cheshire. It played a dominant role in the economy and commerce, as well as the religious life of the area, until the time of dissolution in 1538. Its name, it is said, means 'May God grant it prosperity', which indeed it did enjoy. Most Cistercian monasteries were founded in remote places, and Dieulacres is no exception, for although it is only a short distance as the crow flies from St Edward's Church in Leek, it enjoyed a quiet, secluded spot, away from the busy life of the town. Lying about one mile to the north of Leek, along what is now Abbey Green Road, the abbey stood on the fertile flood plain of the River Churnet. The well-watered meadows supported sheep and cattle, and grew many crops. The flooding problem was alleviated by the construction of a raised causeway, or 'sure-way' above the flood level. The present road follows the same elevated route.

Evidence suggests that the abbey was wealthy and influential, and occupied a position of some status in the Cistercian order. Its treasures were lost to Henry VIII at the Dissolution of the Monasteries, and the abbey was destroyed. Some features of the stonework are incorporated in neighbouring farm buildings and barns, but there is no public access to this protected site.

Let us imagine that we are back in the 14th Century. The grey mist in the valley lies low over the meadows, like a blanket muffling all sound. The river silently glides over its rocky bed. As we cross the sure-way we see, rising above the mist, the impressive structure of the abbey, its columns and arches leading to its lofty vaulted roof, as if reaching towards the sky. If we were able to look more closely we would see fine examples of the craft and skill of the stonemasons in the bases and capitals, buttresses and corbels, tracery and vaulting, for this is a well-built edifice. The massive piers support the arches at the tower crossing. The tower rises above the roof, at the crossing of nave and transepts, like a finger pointing to Heaven. We are not privileged to see the sacristry, chapter house or parlour, nor can we walk in the cloister or visit the monks' day room or dormitory, and the warmth and hospitality of the frater range, refectory and kitchen are also denied to us. Monasteries were very private places. The monks of the Cistercian order adhere faithfully to the simplicity of the monastic life. Apart from their devotions, farming will occupy most of their waking day, and lay brothers are drafted in to help with the work on the land. Work is usually done between the morning chapter meeting and dinner. In the winter this means four hours without a break, and much longer in summer, when a mid-day rest is granted. There are no servants, for the monks and lay brothers run the kitchens and workshops, overseen by the cellarer. Sheep are farmed for their wool, and cattle and crops on the site make the abbey virtually self-sufficient.

We are not privy to the private and personal lives of the inhabitants of the abbey, and can only guess at the internal politics, intrigues and petty jealousies. Within this closed community there will be, in the tangle of human relationships and feelings, love and loathing, passion and hatred, but of these we can only surmise. However, the long day is far spent, so we must leave the monks to their devotions and intrigues, and return to the Twentieth Century.

Ludchurch, Swythamley.

The road to Gradbach

"Swiss" style cottages at Ilam - the gateway to Dovedale

CHAPTER VIII

DOVEDALE

*Alstonefield, Lode Mill, Mill Dale, Dovedale,
Ilam, Blore and Waterhouses*

A CARRIAGE AND PAIR! Nithsdale, my friend, were you getting a little soft, as your journeyings came towards an end? Such luxury, this roomy landau when compared to the bicycle of your earlier trips. However, we shall use our motor car, for we have a long trip, but be warned, my friend, we shall get out and walk at times.

Our route retraces our third outing initially, via Thorncliffe, Morridge and Blakemere to Hulme End. Beyond Hulme End we take the road to Alstonefield. The spelling of the name is a matter for debate - Alstonfield or Alstonefield? The Ordnance Survey map has 'Alstonefield', and if, as W.H.Duigan suggests in his 'Notes on Staffordshire Place Names' (1902), the name derives from the Anglo Saxon *Æne's-stone-field*, we will stick to that, so Alstonefield it is.

Alstonefield is a long straggling village, built high on the ridge on the western hills of the Dove. Though spread over a larger area it is much the same size as Longnor and Hartington, and is very popular with visitors to Dovedale. Its limestone architecture gives it a picturesqueness almost all its own; and the farmsteads, with well kept lawns and pretty flower gardens, add materially to its charms. Its ancient church where Charles Cotton worshipped, is quaint, archaeologically interesting, and rich in wonderfully carved oak pews.

I didn't discover Alstonefield until I had my first motor car. It was way beyond the limits of our boyhood rambles, and there was no bus service. It appears to be a fairly prosperous village; a good place to retire to, as many have discovered for themselves. The houses and cottages are attractive - well appointed without being 'towny', well designed without being too rustic. Well kept and tidy, Alstonefield is one of those traditional villages which could not be found anywhere except in England.

'As I am an honest man, a very pretty church.' This was Isaac Walton's first impression of St Peter's Church at Alstonefield, which he visited with his friend Charles Cotton. The settlement at Alstonefield has a very long history - what the writers of early guide books might refer to as 'a place of great antiquity'. There is clear evidence of Norman architecture in the south doorway and a chancel arch. However, a great feature of the church is its fine Jacobean woodwork. The two-decker pulpit dates from 1637, and there are some splendid box pews. The unique Cotton Pew perpetuates the memory of the great Charles Cotton, but unfortunately, and perhaps misguidedly, this was, at some time in the past, painted in a greenish-grey colour. There is also some good stained glass.

Methodism had some shaky early stirrings at Alstonefield, and it was some time before Non-conformity was strongly established. The Baptists tried and failed, and eventually the Wesleyans, with their house meetings, began to expand and develop. Eventually, in 1824, it became possible to build a handsome chapel, seating 280, which remained in use until its closure in 1981, following the break up of the old Wetton and Longnor Methodist Circuit.

Alstonefield was one of the outlying villages which the Leek and Manifold Light Railway sought to serve, but it was yet another example of how the operators of the railway got their sums wrong. Not only was it too far away from the line geographically to be viable, but their estimates of the expected passenger traffic were wildly out. Out of a total population of about 3,300 in 1891 in this area to the north of the valley it was estimated that 7% would use the railway on Leek Market days, and 3% on the other days of the week, making some 35,000 individual journeys in a single year. In the event, nothing like this figure was reached.

Alstonefield gives us access to the secluded little hamlet of Mill Dale, set down in the upper valley of the River Dove. Millway Lane, a lovely, narrow lane, its grass verges a riot of wild flowers, descends steeply to the river, passing a tiny, stone built chapel which hugs the hillside. This was very much an outpost of the Primitive Methodist movement which spread from Mow Cop through North Staffordshire in the early Nineteenth Century. The movement reached Mill Dale in 1815, when the protestant dissenters met in a house. The little chapel was built in 1835, but always struggled through lack of support in such an isolated spot, with a small resident population, and was absorbed into the Ashbourne Primitive Methodist Circuit in 1886.

Mill Dale is truly a Staffordshire hamlet on the River Dove, which is spanned by a splendid pack-horse bridge, known as Viator's Bridge, in deference to the Isaac Walton and Charles Cotton connection. Our old friend Edward Bradbury has an excellent description of Mill Dale in his book 'All about Derbyshire'. His late-Victorian sentiments are still very relevant, for, apart from motor cars on high days and holidays, the Twentieth Century has had little impact on Mill Dale.

It is a wild and lonely walk, the features of Dove Dale still impressing the scenery, though verdant slopes and more open views obtain as we proceed up the banks of the river:

>   In this romantic region, wandering on,
>   (Where every living thing can stir the mind,)
>   Recurs the bold rock scenery: anon,
>   A rustic bridge appears, and lodged behind,
>   A group of cottages with mill to grind.

This is Mill Dale, more than a mile from the Dove Holes, a small hamlet clothed in green and gray and hidden from the haunts of men. Alstonfield is not far off up among the hills, to the left, but we see nothing of it as we wander on by the side of our loved stream, which comes dancing and laughing to meet us, and nothing distracts the deep seclusion of the Dale.

Bradbury approached Mill Dale from the south, and if you stick to the dale itself, being tempted by the delightful river, where you may see a dipper or a kingfisher, you will miss the surrounding countryside. So typically English, the dry-stone walls and green meadows are the setting for a sprinkling of charming stone-built dwellings with their traditional cottage gardens - none finer than the perfect gem by the roadside as you descend from Hopedale.

MANY WRITERS HAVE WAXED LYRICAL about the delights of Dove Dale and the various dales which link with it. Photographers have captured it in their Canons and Minoltas; artists on their canvases and sketch pads. Calendar and postcard views abound; its images adorn many a kitchen, on aprons and tea towels. It has not escaped the film maker, looking for suitable locations, and videos, foreign to your experience, Nithsdale, are widely available. All this concerted publicity has been a tremendous public relations exercise for Dove Dale, promoting it far and wide, way beyond its capacity to cope with milling throngs. Consequently footpaths have become eroded, wildlife has suffered in the loss of certain habitats and litter can be a problem. The detritus of civilisation has invaded the area to an alarming degree. A broad, stoned path stretches up the dale, alongside the river, installed in the interests of conservation, and providing easy walking for the many who do not wish to get their shoes dirty. But perhaps this 'visitor invasion' is nothing new, for you, my good friend, observed:

> *Then one meets all manner of folk on holiday. There are Londoners sweating and suffering martyrdom in Harris tweeds and highland gaiters; Americans taking the dale like a quick lunch, with a guide book; gay lasses from the Potteries; anglers deprecating the presence of other folk; artists and artistic photographers troubled with the same complaint; wearied but otherwise contented individuals basking in the sunshine; honeymoon couples; honeymoon couples in prospect; and picnic parties galore. In winter 'tis one long solitude, yourself, some sheep perhaps, and the donkeys.*

Nothing has changed, my friend. Perhaps the *'Harris tweeds and highland gaiters'* have given way to jeans and trainers, and the lasses from the Potteries are maybe not so gay, but the crowds still flock to Dove Dale, which has become a tourist honey-pot! This is perhaps not surprising when you realise that about half the population of the country live within 50 miles of Dove Dale, making it accessible to millions for a day out, and the car parks become crowded. However, the further you venture into the heart of the dale, away from the car parks and the famous stepping stones which mark the limit of many peoples' experience of Dove Dale, it becomes relatively quiet and there are times when you will be quite alone. It is then that the true beauty of these magnificent dales becomes fully apparent.

IT'S TIME FOR A STORY OR TWO, and this narrow part of Dove Dale, between Thorpe Cloud and Mill Dale, has a number to offer. Along this section are some splendid rock formations. The Lion Rock is an accurate image of the face of the king of beasts, sculptured by the hand of nature. Ilam Rock and Tissington Spires stark pillars of limestone rising dramatically from the water's edge. Pickering Tor is a craggy rock face, carved into strange shapes. There are a number of caves, like Dove Holes, high and wide, but shallow, and the dramatically shaped Reynard's Cave, perched precariously in the steep valley side.

This is the setting for a number of stories. In July 1761 there occurred the kind of incident that would have delighted today's media, for it involved a clergyman and a young lady. The Rev.W.Langton was with a party, enjoying the delights of the dale. After enjoying a picnic near Reynard's Cave the party decided to return to Tissington. The reverend gentleman decided to ride his horse along a steep and precarious route up the side of the valley. Miss La Roche, a young lady of the party, agreed to accompany him on the same horse. Mistaking the route, the riders followed a sheep track, which gradually became too steep to ascend. In attempting to turn round, the horse slipped and fell. The Rev. Langton was thrown down the rocky face, and was so badly injured that he died a few days later. His young lady companion was saved when her long hair became entangled in a thorn bush, and suffered only minor injuries. But just imagine the headlines in today's tabloid newspapers!

The area around Reynard's Cave is the setting for another, somewhat similar story. Nearby is Sharplow Point, a rocky promontory also known as Lover's Leap, so named because of a previous near-tragedy. A young girl, driven to distraction because she had been jilted by her lover chose the spot for a spectacular suicide attempt. Throwing herself from the height, her fall was broken by the shrubs and bushes and she survived. However, after a second or third attempt, she finally succeeded. Your own matchless prose, Nithsdale, describes the event:

Petticoats parachutically graduated the usual acceleration of sixteen feet per second in one second, and the lady landed on her feet unhurt. A second time she came down with the petticoat

brake triumphant. But at the third attempt, poor thing, she must
have discarded her 'coats or began head first, for tradition hath
it she broke her neck.

A story in Baddeley's Guide to the Peak Distict (1884) tells of
an old hag who lived rent free in a small cave near Mill Dale. When
asked by a visitor where her lavatory was, she replied "Down in't
river." The visitor pursued his questioning, "And when did you last
wash yourself?" to which the old crone replied, "Well, I'm not quite
certain whether it were last summer or t'summer afore."

Lode Mill lies upstream from Mill Dale. As its name suggests,
it was the site of a water mill which remained in operation until the
1930s. The mill buildings still stand. The road formerly crossed by a
ford, and a woman was drowned here in the seventeenth century. It is
now bridged, taking the road from Alstonefield into Derbyshire, and
away from our Staffordshire Moorlands.

ILAM IS A CHARMING VILLAGE, but a nightmare for the makers
of road signs. How do you style its modest little four-letter name
without making it look like 'llam' or 'Ilam'? A typographical
problem which the latest signs seem to have overcome by giving the
second 'L' a small tail. The old Anglo-Saxon spelling of 'Hylum' or
'Hilum' would have been much clearer. The literal meaning is 'a
place in the hills', which indeed it is. But let us not play our lexicon
games with this little village, for it has so much more to offer to the
discerning visitor. I first discovered Ilam many years ago, as a small
boy, at the end of a family ramble. We had walked through Rushley
Woods, into the valley and down to Ilam. My first impression, as I
recall, was that it was a welcome rest for tired young legs, but there
was nothing there! At least, nothing much to interest a small boy!
But then there was the river, and you could always throw stones in a
river, make stone dams, sail log boats, gather frog-spawn or get wet
in several other ways. Alas, though, we still had to walk to the
Ashbourne road to catch the bus home.

A rather more mature impression of Ilam came much later, for
it has many points of interest. The little village school is exactly like
all the village schools of your dreams. Perched on a grassy slope at

the bottom of the hill at the far end of the village, it recalls the halcyon schooldays of a bygone age, when slates were used instead of calculators, blackboards instead of CD Roms, and multiplication tables instead of computers. Records were kept in meticulously hand-written ledgers, registers listed every pupil as an individual, and exercise books garnished with ink blots, represented each child's best efforts. Built in 1854, the neat little building is surmounted by a slender spire housing the school bell, which would summon the children from village and farm to their lessons. Its gables are embellished by ornate barge boards. In perfect symmetry, it is a pure delight, and does not allow itself even to be detracted by the nearby bus garage. The adjoining house, where the school master lived, complements the school building perfectly. The traditional school, with its resident teacher, was always an integral part of village life, and a real sense of community was maintained. Today, the surviving village schools are usually staffed by non-resident teachers, and, worse still from a community point of view, if the school has closed the children are transported to the nearest town by bus! The demise of the village school is an example of the erosion of rural life.

Ilam is a model village, laid out around 1830-1840 by the Watts-Russell family of Ilam Hall. The picturesque Gothic gabled cottages, which have something of a Swiss appearance date from this time, and with their neat gardens, provide a splendid backdrop to the village scene. The Watts-Russells, a wealthy manufacturing family, were typical of the early Victorian 'squirearchy', leaving their mark on the area as a lasting memorial. At the entrance to the village the elegant 'Eleanor Cross' is a memorial to Mrs Watts-Russell. Designed by Gilbert Scott in ornate Gothic style, it was erected in 1840, and incorporated a drinking fountain. But, almost as a statement on Victorian propriety, Ilam has no village pub!

The work of Gilbert Scott can also be seen in the Church of Holy Cross. Much of this dates from the 13th Century, but in 1855 Scott carried out extensive restoration work. Also in the church, and dominating the north side where it stands in a private chapel, is the huge marble memorial, carved by Sir Francis Chantrey in 1831. This depicts the dying moments of David Pike Watts, who lies on his death bed, giving his final benediction to his grieving wife and children. The pure, smooth, white marble gives the statuary an unreal, other-worldly appearance. A rather less spectacular but no less deep mourning is embodied in the simple, sad relics of flowers and white gloves from the coffin of an unmarried girl. Known as maiden garlands, these were traditionally hung in churches following the death of a young maiden. The church also has one of the earliest Norman fonts in England. Rudely carved, it incorporates dragons and crude human figures, the significance of which is not clear.

In the churchyard are two fine Anglo Saxon crosses, both nearly complete, showing birds, human figures and ornamented plait work. The taller cross stands 7 feet high, and the other is 4 feet. These crosses are evidence of the great antiquity of the settlement at Ilam.

Ilam Hall is an elegant mansion, Elizabethan in character, in a curious mixture of architectural styles. A country seat of some eminence, it was re-built in the 1820s for Jesse Watts-Russell. The architect was John Shaw. There was some demolition in the 1930s, when the Hall became a Youth Hostel. Its extensive grounds and idyllic parkland are a great attraction for visitors today, for the estate is now in the care of the National Trust. Once the abode of the privileged few, it is now open to all who care to come. The grounds include the elegant St Bertram's Bridge, which was once a packhorse bridge, and another fragment of a Celtic cross, which Victorian romanticism has rather fancifully named the 'Battle Cross'.

Ilam is not without its literary associations. William Congreve, it is believed, wrote his comedy 'The Old Bachelor' and much of his 'Mourning Bride' in the grounds of Ilam Hall. This would be at the time when the earlier hall was owned by the Port family. Dr Samuel Johnson, who, finding little in the countryside that appealed to him, once remarked that one green field was like another green field. Nevertheless, the Ilam countryside inspired him to write:

Ilam has grandeur tempered with softness; the walker congratulates his own arrival at the place, and is grieved to think he must ever leave it. As he looks up to the rocks, his thoughts are elevated; as he turns his eyes on the valley, he is composed and soothed......Ilam is the fit abode of pastoral virtue, and might properly diffuse its shades over nymphs and swains.

Dr Johnson, it is said, also took Ilam as the inspiration for his 'Happy Valley' when writing 'Rasselas'. In addition, the ubiquitous Cotton and Walton were frequent visitors. Many writers of Victorian guide books also featured Ilam in their works, and wrote glowingly of its charms. And, of course, it did not escape the pen of yourself, my friend:

Ilam, with its unfenced roads, and chalet-like cottages, and its cross to the memory of Mrs. Watts-Russell, almost beggars description. Ilam Church, also unfenced within the grounds of Ilam Hall, and exceedingly ancient, is most interesting, and contains an elaborate mausoleum, Chantrey's masterpiece, representing in marble a Mr Pike Watts on his death-bed giving a last blessing to the family gathered round him. Trespassing further into the beautiful grounds we saw Ilam Hall, and continuing along the path skirting the Manifold, which, by the way, joins the Dove below Ilam, we came to where the subterranean waters of the Manifold and Hamps reappear.

This pathway, my friend, is Paradise Walk, appropriately named, for it is a sheer delight. The underground river comes to the surface through boil holes, gurgling merrily in the spring, when the water is high, more sluggish and drowsy in the heat of summer. It is a sylvan scene, where mixed woodland in many shades of green, verdant meadows sprinkled with wild flowers and sparkling stream blend together in perfect harmony. The fresh green tracery of spring burgeons in the summer sun, with vivid flashes of colour here and there, to become burnished in many shades of red, gold and brown in the autumn, and then to sleep through the cold grip of winter.

Alfred Wainwright, doyen of the Lake District, once said that his beloved Haystacks was a place where a man could lose a persistent headache, or ease a nagging worry. Paradise Walk is just such a place. Truly Nature and Art are wedded together in a blessed union at Ilam.

THE ROAD FROM ILAM climbs steeply, winding and unfenced, to the ancient hamlet of Blore. There are splendid open views down to the picture village we have just left, dominated by the heights of

Thorpe Cloud and Bunster Hill, with the delectable valley of the Dove between. St Bartholomew's Church at Blore has a fine 14th Century tower, with other parts dating from the 15th Century. The interior has some excellent Jacobean woodwork, and an ornate Victorian wrought iron screen. Amongst the memorials the name of Bassett is very prominent. There is a fine brass in memory of a William Bassett who died in 1498. Another William Bassett died in 1601, and his family tomb, including his wife and son-in-law, dominates the north-east area of the church. A number of the old properties in Blore have now become holiday accommodation, housing transitory visitors who come to enjoy the delights of the Dove Dale area which we, my friend, have been sharing.

But now it is time to return to Leek, completing the circle with a visit to nearby Waterhouses.

Two miles of a steep bank downwards, past Miles Knoll, with a magnificent distant panorama before us, and only one turn of any consequence brought us to Waterhouses, prettily situated in the valley of the Hamps, and boasting the southern terminus of the Leek and Manifold Valley Light Railway. It is a most indefinite village, with houses, many substantial and even imposing, dotted daintily, some on one side and some on the other of the river bed, and a double row sembling of a street at each end. Space was evidently no object when Waterhouses was laid out. Leaving Waterhouses we traversed a mile and a half of uninteresting road to Winkhill. The waters of the Hamps here were in striking contrast to the dry condition of the bed below Waterhouses. Thence we journeyed leisurely up New Street, recalling Friday's thunderstorm; and continuing as before, but in greater comfort, by Berkhamsytch, Bottomhouse, and Bradnop, we duly arrived in Leek.

Nithsdale's Grindon snowscene

The modest source of the mighty River Trent, Biddulph Moor

CHAPTER IX

OUR FINAL OUTING

Longsdon, Dunwood, Endon, Gratton, Lask Edge,
Biddulph Moor, Horton and Rudyard

OUR TIME TOGETHER is getting short, Nithsdale, but there are still a few more parts of the Staffordshire Moorlands to explore before we are done, and I propose to combine your last two outings into one. Our journey today will take us almost to the fringe of the industrial Potteries, indeed some of the places we shall visit owe more allegiance to the Potteries than they do to the Moorlands. Our route will take us into the Upper Trent Valley and the source of that great river which links so many cities, towns and industries on its way to the Humber Estuary and the North Sea.

Before we broaden our horizons, however, let us take the road from Leek which follows Broad Street, passing the site of the old railway station, and leaves the town along the Newcastle Road.

Beyond the Churnet we toiled up Ladderedge bank, and by the brickyard, as well as from the summit, had another glorious glimpse of the beautiful panorama of Leek, which from this height seems to be laid at the base of the distant Roches.

We reach the village of Longsdon, a mixture of the ancient and modern. The oldest properties are probably Stanlowe, Bradshaw and Dunwood. According to our friend Mr Sleigh, Leek's venerable historian, Ralph de Stanlowe was a warrior under Edward the First, Walter de Stanlowe served Edward the Second and Richard the Second and Robert is mentioned in a deed of 1431. Stanlowe, or Stonelow Hall is an Elizabethan stone-built property, on the site of an earlier 13th Century house, with some evidence of a Saxon burial mound nearby. Nearby is another old property, Bradshaw, and John Rode of Bradshaw is named as a trustee to John Rothwell of Leek in a document dated August 14th 1619. Dunwood is mentioned in a subsidy roll of the time of Edward the Third. The present Dunwood

Hall, which you mention, my friend, is a gaunt Victorian Gothic house, dating from 1870.

In the Longsdon area we find the earliest reference to Methodism in the Leek area. Bryan's Hay, an old farmhouse on the left, where the old road joins the new, was a meeting house for the early Methodists, but the date when the first flame was kindled there is not known. It would be prior to 1754, for at that time the family named Hammersley, who were pioneers of the work at Bryan's Hay, went to live in Leek. A Wesleyan Chapel was built in Longsdon in 1870, but, like many village chapels, it has now been closed for worship and converted to a house. 'Suitable for conversion' has become a bit of a cliché with estate agents when selling old chapels! Modern Longsdon consists of the desirable houses and detached villas which line the main road and the two roads leading down to the canal. Mainly owned by business and professional people, this 20th Century development has given the village some status in the local housing market. Even the Anglican Church, St Chad's, is 20th Century. It was built in 1903-5 to the design of Gerald Horsley, reflecting the style of Norman Shaw, and finding much inspiration from Shaw's All Saints Church in Leek.

TRADITION AND MODERNITY are even more apparent in Endon. Sprawling, spreading, expanding Endon is almost a suburb of the Potteries, for you are now aware of an urban landscape all the way to the city. Many Endon residents work in the Potteries, commuting daily to business, fuming in frustration along that six mile stretch of traffic-snarled, temper-fraying road, inching slowly forwards. Oh! for the freedom of our high moors, WH, for here the twentieth century is closing all too tightly around us.

But Endon still has its old heart, and much tradition remains. The stone cottages by the ford, the old chapel, the well, forge and shop cluster together, almost a village within the wider village, as it were. Indeed, this area is known simply as 'The Village'. Normally a quiet little corner, away from the busy main road, the old village comes to vibrant life, like Brigadoon, once a year, at the Spring Bank Holiday weekend, when the traditional well dressing ceremony takes place. Well dressing is normally regarded as a Derbyshire custom, but this little outlier in North Staffordshire has been taking place each year since 1845. At one time there were a number of other well dressings at towns and villages in Staffordshire, but Endon appears to be the sole survivor. Prior to 1845 the old village of Endon had been in need of a fresh water supply, and a local man, Thomas Heaton, tapping the water from a nearby spring, built a substantial structure around the well, and very generously presented it to the village. When the well was completed and the water connected up, it was felt that there ought to be some kind of ceremony to mark the occasion. A villager named Philip Rogers offered to decorated the well for the occasion, and as the ceremony was to take place on Oak Apple Day, May 29th, the decorations consisted of the branches of oak trees. Oak Apple Day commemorates the escape of King Charles II, when he hid in the oak tree at Boscobel. Nowadays the decorations follow the Derbyshire practice of using sheets of wet clay laid on boards, into which are pressed mosses, leaves, flower petals, seeds and other natural materials of different colours and textures, pushed into the clay with great skill, to form a picture illustrating the theme for the year, usually a national anniversary or perhaps a Biblical subject.

In the early days the well dressers were paid a wage of 2s 6d per day, with an allowance for bread, cheese and beer. In 1868 the bill for these refreshments was £2 4s 8d. In later years these concessions ceased, and the work is now voluntary. Thus, in 1845, a tradition was born which has survived two world wars and all the other vicissitudes of the present century. The primary origins of well dressing lie in the ancient pagan practice of worshipping water gods and spirits, known as 'welpeonthunza' or well worship. Today the emphasis is laid on the ceremony as a thanksgiving to God for the gift of water, and so the Christian church has become involved, and a religious service is a central act in the celebrations.

To be chosen as Well Dressing Queen is an honour which many young girls in the village aspire to, and this memory is usually cherished throughout their life. The Queen is traditionally crowned four times, once on Saturday afternoon following the church service, again on Saturday evening and twice on Bank Holiday Monday. Endon Well Dressing attracts thousands of visitors each year. It is another of those splendid local family outings. As a boy, I associated the idea of well dressing with people being well dressed, so that when the promise of "going to see the well dressing" was made I had a vision of crowds of people parading around dressed in their finery, which I would have found rather boring. The fun fair, however, with its amusements, stalls and sideshows was a much more exciting proposition. The festivities are usually centred around the main well and the smaller well, which is traditionally dressed by a junior. Morris dancers perform their time-honoured routines, and other events, including sports, maypole dancing, competitions and band performances take place on the field, which is singularly known as the Jaw-bone Field.

A village with traditions such as Endon will always have its share of 'characters'. In spite of the great influx of commuter residents, there are still a number of families in the village whose roots can be traced back hundreds of years. The headstones in the churchyard honour their memory, and their names figure prominently in any recorded history of Endon. One such village worthy, who died at the age of 104, was known as 'Billy Willet o' th' Eaves'. It was his great boast that, at a very advanced age, he and another old man performed a feat of endurance that would have been daunting for a much younger man - long-distance dancing. Bragging that he was still hale and hearty, he would proudly relate how, "We begun th' dance at Mester Ford's o' Yen-Bonk abait seven o' clock at neet on th' second o' September, an' we nivver stopt whoile dayleet on th' fourteenth!" There is, of course, a catch in wily Willie's amazing claim, for the dance took place at a village merrymaking in 1752, the year in which the change was made in the calendar from the old style to the new, and the 3rd of September that year was reckoned as the 14th. Thus, Willie's feat was reduced from 12 days to as many hours! A somewhat paradoxical epitaph is found on the stone in memory of William Murhall, a member of an old Staffordshire family, who died in 1762. His headstone records:

> Part of what I possessed is left to others
> And what I gave away remains to me.

Graveyards are not without their little paradoxes, and often provide a rich field for the study of epigrams.

LET US NOW LEAVE ENDON, my friend, and follow the road by the well to Gratton, a scattered community which has neither church nor pub, but does have a little wayside chapel.

Gratton is a pastoral locality, with a most elaborate maze of pretty lanes. It cannot be called a village, and as it seemed well nigh impossible to find two houses in close proximity I am afraid to call it a hamlet .... We climbed still upwards from among Gratton's fertile grass lands, through a purely agricultural countryside resounding with the rattle of the mowing machine, where everyone seemed to be employed in the hay fields, by Blackwood Hill to Lask Edge and the barren heights of Biddulph Moor.

BIDDULPH MOOR is sufficiently close to Biddulph and the northern towns of the Potteries to give people living in those parts a taste of the real moorlands. There is a rocky outcrop of gritstone, Wicken Stones, to complete the scene, as if the moorland scenery is doing its best to make inroads into the northern fringe of the Potteries. Biddulph Moor, or 'Biddle Mooer', as the locals would say, is wild and gritty, a working community where chapel and pub have welded the social life of the area from the time when the mines and the ironworks welded the working life of the people. There were many more pubs in the area in those days than we see today. Biddulph Moor's close proximity to Mow Cop meant that Primitive Methodism made an early impact on the area, and the pioneer 'ranters' of the movement came with their fiery brand of preaching and established chapels and camp meetings in these northern hills.

Like most closely-knit communities, Biddulph Moor folk have a certain wit and repartee. A story recorded on Joseph Castles' History of Biddulph tells how a youth walking with his sweetheart on Biddulph Moor came upon a local man riding a donkey. To impress his young lady companion he thought he would take a rise out of the local fellow, and asked him what he would sell his donkey for. Much to the amusement of the young lady, the reply, in the vernacular, was: "Why dust want t'know? Is thee feyther sellin' thee, or is he thinkin' o' keepin' two donkeys?"

Another story, found in the Rev.J.B.Dyson's history of

Methodism in the Congleton circuit, tells of a visiting preacher given hospitality with a local family. On his arrival at the cottage he was welcomed with the words, "Come on in. We've got a nice piece o' beef boilin' in th'pot, but its gotten so big we conna get it out. We hav'na got a fork. We 'ad a fork once, but our Ben lost it!"

A legend, which the inhabitants of Biddulph Moor have not always taken kindly to, recounts that Herbert de Langtry, returning from the Crusades at the time of Richard I, brought with him a group of Saracen captives. These were said to be of both sexes, and they settled in Biddulph Moor. Their descendants over many generations, almost a breed apart, were swarthy, wild and gypsy-like in their appearance, and introduced words of Arabic origin into the local dialect. Other evidence suggests that this darkly handsome breed were more likely descendants of the ancient Brigantian people. In any event, they are a hardy, independent, no nonsense, nonconformist breed, ardent followers of football (Port Vale, of course), fervent for their cricket at nearby Knypersley and devoted to their gardens, their church and their chapel!

SO LET US HEAD TOWARDS KNYPERSLEY my friend, for we are seeking the source of the River Trent - 'the smug and silver Trent', as Shakespeare put it. For a river which rises in the Staffordshire Moorlands, and follows its 170-mile course to the North Sea, passing through some of our greatest cities and finest countryside, its actual source is somewhat modest. There is a complex arrangement of headwaters in the area between Biddulph Moor and Knypersley Reservoir. There are many springs and wells in the area, and the Ordnance Survey map can be confusing when seeking the actual source of the Trent. 'Head of Trent' is marked to the south of the reservoir, where the infant Trent has become a distinct stream, but about two miles to the north is Trent Head Farm. It is near here, almost hidden in the fields between Leek Lane and New Street, that the real source is found. In 1935 Biddulph Urban District Council decided that this was it, and the Staffordshire Moorlands District Council have endorsed this by marking and naming the site in 1996.

You approach from a cul-de-sac, take a grassy path to a

footbridge, cross the bridge and there, diagonally across the field, in a slight dip, is the Head of the Trent - according to the local authority, that is, so I guess we must settle for this. And having seen the great river safely on its way to the sea, let us turn towards Leek, over the high road on Lask Edge, and descend to the quiet little village of Horton.

You cannot think of the Horton and Gratton area without thinking of George Heath, the Moorlands Poet. Genius is a word that is often used lightly nowadays, but there is both rarity and permanence in true genius. Sometimes genius finds its source in the most humble surroundings, and takes root in common soil. Such genius is found in poets like Robert Burns, who, though poor, managed to escape one of the worst evils of poverty - illiteracy. Such genius is found in George Heath. The eldest son of a large family, he was born on 9th March 1844 at Hall Gate Farm, Gratton, in the parish of Horton. His parents were small farmers who worked hard to eke out a modest living. Young George attended the National School at Horton, where he learned the basics of reading and writing. His religious instruction was gained at Endon Wesleyan Sunday School, where the Superintendent was his relative and namesake, George Heath. During his youth George worked long, hard hours on the farm, but in due course he became apprenticed to a local joiner and builder, Samuel Heath of Gratton. As his experience broadened he began to develop a real thirst for learning. The rural nature of Gratton, however, was barren ground to nurture this new-found yearning for scholarship, and his bucolic companions and family were too unlearned to be of much practical help. Books were not readily available, and it was providential that he developed a friendship with a young Endon man of his own age, Herbert W. Foster. Foster had received a good education at Alleyne's Grammar School, Uttoxeter, where he had access to a well stocked library. The two young men had much in common with each other; they both had a deep love for nature and the countryside, and enjoyed intellectual conversation. The broadening of George Heath's mind was greatly enhanced by this friendship, although Foster had a leaning towards art, while Heath's poetic proclivities were beginning to blossom.

Foster went on to gain a National Art Scholarship at South

Kensington. The development of George Heath as a poet was as much a spiritual experience as a literary one, and his inner nature spoke with a new voice to him. Many of his early poems throb with this new life and hope. However, as is all too frequent, genius became tarnished by the stroke of tragedy. In 1864, towards the end of his apprenticeship, he was working on the restoration of Horton Church when he suffered a severe cold. This developed into consumption - the disease which ultimately was to bring his young life to a tragic, premature end. Too ill to work, his enforced invalidity gave him time to read, write and study in earnest. This grim period was perhaps the most productive for his creative poetic talents. He was tutored in the study of Latin and Greek by the Rev. James Badnall, the vicar of Endon. He mastered these languages, and made a translation of Virgil's 'Aeneid'. He also studied ancient and English history, and his disciplined use of time left him free to study mathematics on Saturdays! Botany was dear to his heart, he confessed to being "a true lover of nature", but "miserably deficient in the minutiae...The flowers are all of them beautiful faces looking up at me; but though familiar to me in one sense, they are not familiar inasmuch as I do not even know their names."

George Heath was an avid reader. All the great classical and contemporary English poets were studied assiduously, and the quality of his poetry was greatly enhanced by this broadening of his knowledge. Alongside this, Heath had a deep and abiding love for the local countryside, as his poem inspired by Rudyard illustrates:

> How sublimely grand the picture
>   Stretching out before my gaze;
> Deluged with the glowing splendour
>   Of the sun's declining rays,
>
> Lies the lake in tranquil beauty,
>   Like a model mimic sea,
> Like a brightly polished mirror,
>   In a frame of ebony;
>
> Like a flood of molten silver,
>   Froth of gold and sapphire dipped,
> Flashing back the efflorescence
>   Of the summer's blazing light.

And away, far up the valley,
　　Rising from the sunlit tide,
Towering hills in stately grandeur,
　　Bound the view on either side.

Turning, twisting, undulating,
　　Sinking low or peaking high,
Throwing up a jaggy outline,
　　Quaintly cut against the sky.

He was a life-long member of the Wesleyan Methodist Society at Endon, where he worshipped regularly as long as he was able. His deep Christian faith was a great source of comfort and strength to him in his infirmity. In his later verse he is obliged to recognise the inevitable, and his subsequent submission to the will of the Creator is made clear in his last utterings in verse:

　　　　　　　Oh! wearisome
And long is life - bold, friendless, hopeless, bad!
How sweet is sleep when one is wearied out!
How sweet is death when one is gone to aye!
Methinks that I could sleep upon the crest
Of any restless wave, as did my master
Upon the raging sea of Galilee -
I am so tired; come to me, gentle sleep!

As if his terminal illness was not enough to bear, cruel fate struck a second tragic blow, like a two-edged sword, on the life of George Heath. He had fallen in love with a girl known only to us as Jenny, and she proved unfaithful. The agony and pain of this broken first love caused him great grief, and haunted much of his later poetry. An extract from his diary brings out, in touching terms, the intensity of his feelings:

February 26th, 1868

Today I have brought down and committed to the flames a batch of letters that I received from a love that was once as a life to me - such letters - yet the writer in the end deserted me. O, the anguish I suffered! I had not looked at them for three years, and opened the portrait of the woman I loved so much, I could scarcely keep back the bitter tears. O, Jenny, the bitterness you caused me will never be obliterated from my heart.

"A broken clue ...."
The grave of George Heath, the Moorland Poet, Horton Churchyard

It seems clear that the ardour of the love which George Heath had for his beloved Jenny transcended mere sexual attraction, being more spiritual than physical - an intensity of passion which perhaps few experience without consummation. It was certainly a love that, for some reason, Jenny did not return, and the cruel rejection broke his heart. In a fine poem, written when consumption and unrequited love had wrecked his young life, he cries

> O God! how intensely and madly I loved,
> How wildly I worshipped that beautiful one;
> You know how inconstant and faithless she proved,
> How basely she left me when summer was gone.

George Heath's illness became terminal towards the end of 1868, when his doctor gave him no hope of recovery. We can picture him in his modest little room in the cottage at Gratton, coughing his life away, his heart broken and his creative talent cruelly snuffed out, like a brief candle. He died on 5th May 1869, aged twenty five years. His grave is in Horton churchyard, marked by a fine Runic cross made to the design of his friend Herbert Foster. The moving inscription is an enigmatic, brief biographical statement, and a tribute which says:

> Erected in Memory
> of GEORGE HEATH of Gratton
> Who, with few aids,
> Developed in these Moorlands
> Poetic powers of great promise,
> But who, stricken by consumption
> After five years suffering,
> Fell a victim to that disease
> May 5, 1869, aged 25 years

> His life a fragment - a broken clue -
> His harp had a musical string or two,
> The tension was great, and they sprang and flew,
> And a few brief strains - a scattered few -
> Are all that remain to mortal view
> Of the marvellous song the young man knew.

A SAD AND TRAGIC STORY, WH, but let us not finish our journeyings on a note of melancholy. That would be a pity, after our splendid days together around the Moorlands, our yarns and our stories, our memories and recollections of bygone days. So let us return to Leek via Rudyard, and revive reminiscences of happy days by the lakeside, of sailing on the lake, of amusements and walks in the woods, of the excitement of railway trips and of those sun-bronzed crowds at Freshwater. And if we hurry back along the Macclesfield Road, my friend, we might just be in time to catch the last few overs of the day at Highfield, before the Umpire calls "Time!"

ENVOI.

As I write these last few pages, my dear Nithsdale, a comet has appeared in the star spangled night sky over the Staffordshire Moorlands. It is visible from the heights of the Roches, the high moors of Morridge, the hills and the dales, the river valleys, the farms, the towns and the old village streets. Its light has taken thousands of years to reach us. It will not return again for another 2000 years. A block of rock and ice 25 miles across, it is a mere 123 million miles distant from Earth! Faced with this immensity of time and space, my friend, leads me to think how infinitesimal is the span of time between your generation and mine, and how puny indeed we are. And because the Moorlands we have been seeking together is something deep within us, it has been possible to bridge the gap between your time and mine, and re-live these grand outings, savouring afresh the incomparable atmosphere of the delectable Highlands of Staffordshire. The moorland area we have travelled is far, far removed from gridlocked traffic jams, bypasses, traffic calming, one-way systems, ring roads, industrial parks, infrastructure, planning laws, ring fencing, spin doctors, sound bites, tele-cottages, theme parks, shopping malls, corporate images, urban renewal, rural decline, leisure centres, factory farming, silos, pollution, pesticides, caravan parks, footpath erosion, river contamination, mass hikes, satellite TV dishes and political correctness. Enough!

"Sufficient still for one day..............", as you said yourself, my dear, dear friend, so I think we will just leave it at that!

A N & J M BOULD

Butchers & Pie Makers

Selected beef, lamb and pork from local farms and markets.
Home made sausages, bacon and fresh poultry. Freshly baked
pies from our own bakery.

Discount on bulk buys for your freezer.
Main stockist in Leek for

54 Derby Street, Leek, Staffs ST13 5AJ
tel. 01538 384334

THE SHIP INN
WINCLE
Nr Macclesfield
Cheshire SK11 0QE

A delightful old country inn set in the hills on the Cheshire/Staffordshire border, the Ship Inn offers warm hospitality, delicious food and fine wines and ales.

Open all the year round but closed on Mondays from November to March inc. Small parties catered for.

For further details contact:
Andrew Harmer & Penny Hinchcliffe
tel. 01260 227217

BURY & HILTON

Estate Agents and Valuers
Chartered Surveyors

6 Market Street Leek Staffordshire ST13 6HZ
Tel: 01538 383344   Fax: 01538 371314
20 Market Place Ashbourne Derbyshire DE6 1EF
Tel: 01335 300181   Fax: 01335 300671
12 Moorland Road Burslem Stoke-on-Trent
Tel: 01782 575297
11 Concert Place, Buxton, Derbys, SK17 6EB
Tel: 01298 27524

STOCKWELL WINES

LEEK

We stock a wide range of Beers, Wines & Spirits
Tel. 01538 371505.................Fax 01538 266785

PICTURE BOOK

Our main shop is in Stanley Street, just down from

BOOKS
GREETING CARDS
FRAMING
ORIGINAL ART

On our second floor we
have a gallery
specialising in original
watercolours of the area
and custom framing.

Woolworths.

Tel 01538 384337 Fax 01538 399696

PICTURE BOOK 2

Specialist book and print shop in Getliffes Yard off Derby Street
Over 2000 Old and Ephemera Prints. Beautiful Greeting Cards
Wrapping Paper. Loose Writing Paper
Bird and Natural History Books
Biography and Transport Books
Fax/phone/ansaphone 01538 3872961
E-mail Ginnypicbook@compuserve.com

Every year is a bonus year
with Britannia.

As one of Britain's leading mutual building societies, Britannia not only
offer you outstanding financial products but also the unique Members'
Loyalty Bonus Scheme. This means we can share
our success with our Members in the form
of a Bonus Payment paid out each and
every year.

For more information on our
Members' Loyalty Bonus Scheme
pop into your local Britannia branch

The Sharing Society

Britannia Building Society Britannia House Leek Staffordshire ST13 5RG